A N

Shipwrecks and Tragedies in the St. John's Narrows

by Rosalind Power

Jeff Blackwood & Associates
St. John's, Newfoundland
2000

Published by:

JEFF BLACKWOOD & ASSOCIATES
c/o 18 Hopeall Street St. John's, Newfoundland A1E 5R3
Telephone/Facsimile: (709) 364-7277

Design/Layout: City Design

Cover Artwork: Joey Power

Canadian Cataloguing in Publication Data

Power, Rosalind, 1944-
A narrow passage: shipwrecks and tragedies in the St. John's Narrows

Includes index.
ISBN 0-9686492-0-3

1. Marine accidents--Newfoundland--St. John's Region--History--19th century. I. Title.

FC2170.S5P69 2000 363.12'3'09718109034 C99-901678-4
G525.P69 2000

CONTENTS

A NARROW PASSAGE

INTRODUCTION

This book is a compilation of over 200 incidents; accidents, drownings, near drownings, etc., which have occurred in and near the St. John's Harbour Narrows up to 1899. Information was gathered from newspapers, Colonial Records and books about St. John's. The major source was *The Royal Gazette* from 1810 - 1900 and *The Evening Telegram* from 1879 - 1900.

The great number of drownings (over ninety people) and wrecks documented in this book shows the dangers our ancestors faced when travelling by sea. No doubt, many minor incidents were not reported by local papers. Also, there are missing issues of some papers covering large tracts of time. More events are recorded starting around 1879 when *The Evening Telegram* was first published. *The Evening Telegram* was a daily paper whereas *The Royal Gazette* only published weekly.

A map has been included on page 21 to show the reader where the rocks, bays, headlands, etc., mentioned in this book are located.

The appendices list many more accidents which have not been covered in the main body of this book plus other interesting events.

I would like to thank Joseph B. Power for many of the sketches in this book. Joey's grandfather, Leo Power was light keeper at Fort Amherst from 1943-1972.

Revelation 20:13 *And the sea gave up the dead which were in it.....*

*A picture of the Narrows taken from a postcard (*CNS*)*

The Narrows; Aptly Named

The St. John's Narrows is only 900 feet wide at the entrance and it narrows to 400 feet near Chain Rock. It was the main point of entry for most people and goods from the earliest history of our island up until the advent of modern transportation. It is truly an unique entrance as a traveller approaching the harbour would see only a solid wall of rock until nearly upon the opening, surely an intimidating sight! And once near the gateway to St. John's, it was not all clear sailing as the narrow channel was peppered with hidden rocks and shoals. Adding to the danger of the earliest seafarers was the lack of lights, pilots or reliable charts to guide them in. On a stormy day and in nighttime, the running of this gauntlet, must have made even the bravest soul tremble with fear.

Sir Richard Henry Bonnycastle had this to say about the entrance in 1842;

"The view on entering the harbour from the ocean, particularly after a very long voyage, is extremely fine. The ship, passing the open roadstead, or one-sided Bay of St. John's, scarcely sees the extremely narrow pass in the high land which she must make, and on entering the Narrows, she has nearly half a mile of intricate navigation before she opens the whole harbour.

On entering, she has, on her right hand, a precipice of sandstone and slate rock, nearly perpendicular, to the height of three hundred feet, above which, almost as steep, frowns the citadel called Signal Hill, a very narrow crest, five hundred and ten feet above the ocean waters. The Narrows themselves are only nine hundred feet across at their sea-face, and diminish to about four; so that from the deck, in passing, one looks up to batteries upon batteries frowning in the sky, or on the edge of perpendicular cliffs, from which a stone might, as it were, be thrown on board.

On the left, the mountain is above six hundred feet in altitude, broken, abrupt, and very picturesque, admitting, however, near the water of a sort of shoulder of small elevation, bristled with dangerous rocks, and shewing again batteries nearer the water's edge, with a jutting promontory of solid rock, on which the Atlantic ever beats in hollow roar, and on which there is a formidable work, with the harbour-light perched on the top of a vaulted barrack.

As soon as the vessel comes abreast of this work, which is on the left entrance of the Narrows, she is hailed by the artillerymen on duty at the signal-post there; and those merchantmen accustomed to the rules of the place, put a board over their quarter, or chalk on it the number of days they have been on their voyage, or their name, if they carry no distinguishing flag, for most of the traders do............"[1]

One of the earliest accidents occurred on April 3,1583 when Sir Humphrey Gilbert approached St. John's harbour with his four ships, the *Delight, Swallow, Squirrel* and *Golden Hind.* Gilbert had come to claim Newfoundland for the British under authority of Queen Elizabeth. At first the merchants refused to admit him for they suspected that he might be a pirate. However, when Gilbert convinced them of his authority, he was permitted to enter. While entering, the *Delight* ran aground on Cahill's Rock on the south side of the harbour much to the embarrassment of the captain for there were 36 ships in the harbour from Britain, Portugal and Spain. A flotilla of boats got together and towed her off and all four vessels anchored safely inside.

The ill-fated *Delight*, was later lost at Sable Island, drowning 85 people in one of Canada's first marine disasters on August 29,1583.[2]

St. John's Narrows from sea, c., 1830 (Joey Power)

A Narrow Channel Fraught with Danger

The first shipping incident near the Narrows mentioned in *The Royal Gazette,* May, 1810 concerned the brig, *Swift.* Note the letter *f* substitutes for the letter *s* in early writings. Here's what the paper wrote about it;

> "The Brig Swift, George Raymond, mafter, from St. John's, New-Brunfwick, with an afforted Cargo of Pork, Flour, Bread, Lumber, &c. In coming into this port on Tuesday evening laft unfortunately fruck a piece of Ice, in her ftarboard bow, and fuddenly filled with water-the mafter and crew however, were taken on board the Sch'r Mary-Ann, Capt. Beattey (then in company) and brought on fhore. Early the next morning, Capt. Raymond went in purfuit of the Brig, and immediately after additional help was procured from the Men of War, &c. who fucceeded in towing her into the harbour in the courfe of the fame day."[3]

Later, on December 20, 1810, a new brig, *Canada*, got all the way from Bermuda to the Pancake Rock where she grounded and was bilged [fill with water]. Captain Thomas Whitney was not the blame as she had a pilot on board and the weather was favourable. The papers stated that there was hopes of raising her. The local people must have seized the opportunity for salvage as a week later a notice appeared in the paper signed John Dunscombe & Co. He warned any persons who had saved any of the materials from the brig to deliver it to the company's wharf, "on pain of prosecution".[4]

A year later, there were three shipwrecks reported in the Narrows. On December 4, 1811, a large Western boat from Paradise, laden with fish and oil, struck the North Head and sunk instantly. Unfortunately, a man, woman and child were drowned while one other passenger and the crew were saved. Four men who tried to save the people from drowning that morning were later awarded for their, " extraordinary exertions" by the Merchant's Society.[5] It was resolved to give a silver medal to John Roche plus he and the other three men, John Keefe, James Keefe and Michel Maher would receive two guineas each from the funds of the Society. These men were probably the military men stationed at Amherst's Tower, later known as Fort Amherst. The men there were involved in other rescues over the years.

Less than two weeks later, on Monday morning, December 16th, 1811, the schooner *Betsey* struck on the opposite side of the Narrows. The vessel was bound from Sydney with coal and provisions for St. John's. When she struck the Southern Head, Captain Manwaring and one man drowned.[6]

The excitement of that tragedy had barely died down when another vessel had an accident in the Narrows. On Friday, December 20th, 1811, the brig *Edgell* struck on Pancake Rock while coming into the harbour. The vessel was carrying a valuable cargo of dry goods and materials from London. Part of the cargo was lost when she bilged but Captain Holmes and crew were not hurt.[7]

Pancake Rock, Prosser's Rock and Chain Rock would prove to be the demise of many vessels down through the years. To get into the harbour of St. John's, sailing vessels could tack in (follow a zigzag course), which caused them to come dangerously close to the rocks and shoreline. If a vessel misstayed, (sails not answer) she would be certain to hit a shoal or rock which so often happened in the Narrows. Besides tacking in, a vessel could warp in. This meant being pulled along by ropes attached to some object such as a buoy, anchor, dock or ring bolts in the rocks.

A Fledgling Pilot Service

When the only means of transportation to St. John's was by sea, the shipping traffic in and out the harbour was very heavy. *The Royal Gazette* published weekly, announced on May 27, 1813 that since its last edition, upwards of 100 sail of vessels have entered the port from Europe. Many of these vessels were having difficulty getting in and out of port.

The leading citizens of St. John's began to realize something had to be done about all the accidents in the Narrows. Therefore, the local merchants took measures to make shipping safer for vessels entering and leaving St. John's harbour. In 1812, a committee consisting of merchants Wm. B. Thomas, Samuel Bulley and N. W. Hoyles, placed notices in the *Royal Gazette.* One ad notified the public that a white buoy had been placed over Prosser's Rock which was not to be used for warping or mooring. Underneath their names was "Pilot's Committee".[8]

Another notice mentioned the harbour pilots. St. John's now had boats fitted out for piloting ships and men were engaged as pilots. However, some of these men were not capable of doing the job of piloting for one notice talked about ships coming to port damaged due to the "ignorance of men taking charge of them as pilots." Therefore, the committee gave notice that men who wished to be pilots would have to be examined before receiving a certificate enabling them to take charge of a ship.[9] One successful man was John Hearn who operated a fish market on Water Street. He offered his services as a pilot in March 1813 by placing an ad in *The Royal Gazette* stating that he was ready at all times night or day to attend with kedges, warps and other necessary articles for that purpose.[10] Two years later he was "launched into eternity" on the Barrens of St. John's for the murder of his wife.[11]

A pilot was blamed for the loss of the schooner *Vulture* in August 1812. Writing from St. John's to home office, W. Haynes informed the owners that their vessel was loss due to the pilot's impudence in attempting to beat through the Narrows. In going about, he went to the South Side and lodged upon a point of rock. The ship was stuck there for three days and was dislodged with great difficulty. All the Guernsey captains in port and 120 men from the H.M.S. *Antelope* succeeded in saving the cargo but it took 30 days to get all the masts and rigging ashore. The writer suggested abandoning the hull. Further correspondence showed that the *Vulture* was salvaged, sold and sailed away to England.[12]

Later, in November there were two groundings in the Narrows. On Friday evening, November 6, 1812, the ship *Maria*, Capt. Cowley, fully laden for Demarara with 6000 quintals of fish, struck on Chain Rock while leaving port. The shock caused the ship's bow to pitch towards the southward. Before the ship answered the helm, she struck again on the south side of the Narrows. This caused her to bilge, her bowsprit was carried away and she sunk at her anchors about an hour later. All attempts to save the vessel was hopeless but happily, no lives were lost.

Two days after, on a Sunday night, the H. M. S. *Avenger,* a 18 gun sloop, became a total wreck in the Narrows. Captain V. Johnston and his 80 man crew were returning from a cruise and while coming in the channel, the wind blew the warship abreast of Chain Rock where she struck hard. Although immediate assistance was given, she received too much damage and could not be rescued.[13] Luckily, there was no loss of life.

As seen in Appendix 1, at least seven or eight ships had met their demise in the Narrows between 1813-1815. The boats and crews mentioned in one rescue were probably the pilot boats and pilots of St. John's; the term "pilot boat" was not used at that time. The pilotage system was still not satisfactory to the merchants it seems because the following notice appeared in the paper on November 30, 1815;

> "Notice: From the great Abuse of the Recommendations given by us to Men who undertake the Piloting of Vessels in and our of this Port, We hereby give this Public Notice, That we no longer authorize any Person or Persons to make use of such a Recommendation bearing our signatures. (Signed) Newman W. Hoyles, William B. Thomas, Nicholas Gill."[14]

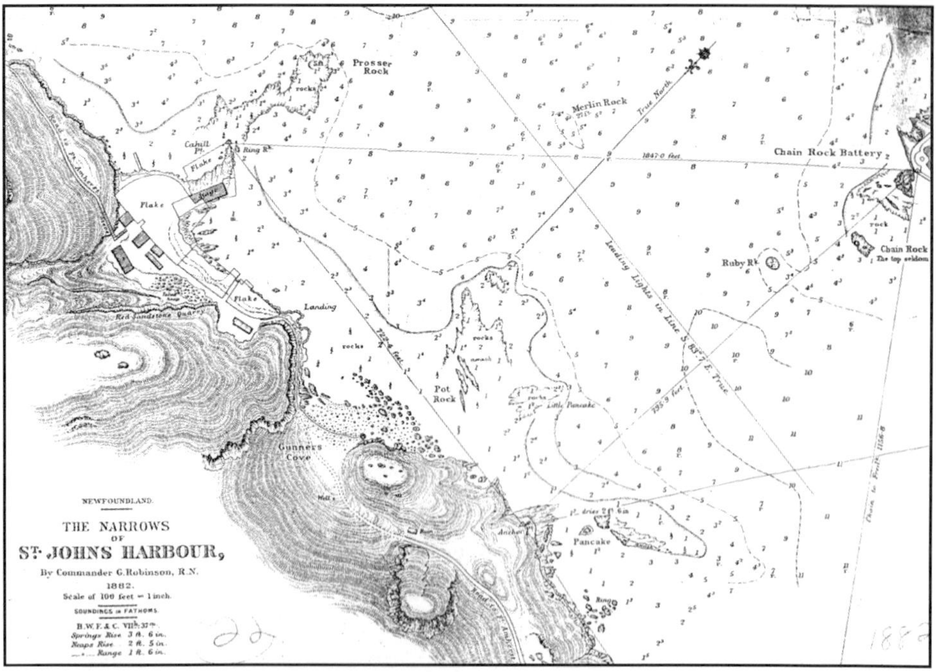

An 1882 map showing rocks in the Narrows near Chain Rock (CNS)

A Hard Night at Sea

Many vessels approached the Narrows after a long journey only to be driven back to sea before gaining the entrance to the inner sanctum that the harbour of St. John's afforded. One such incident occurred on October 9, 1816. On Tuesday, Master Costello and crew in the schooner *Success*, left Cape Broyle with a load of fish in the hold and casks of oil on deck and arrived at the Narrows Wednesday afternoon. They got in as far as the outer buoy when the southeasterly wind suddenly chopped round to north north west. The wind increased strongly to hurricane proportions accompanied by a heavy fall of snow. The Narrows was a very dangerous place to be in such violent weather. The anchor was let go but didn't hold so the cable was slipped and the crew started to put the sail up as the vessel was now drifting dangerously close to shore. Before they could raise the sail, she drove on the south point of the harbour and bilged. After striking several times, she got clear of the rocks but now there was three feet of water in the hold and most of the sails were torn to pieces. There was no choice but to put to sea and run before the wind. It was a gloomy prospect for the men especially when they had been so near to safety for they knew they were in for a hard night at sea. Wednesday night as the crew struggled at sea to save themselves and their vessel, a terrible storm raged. Throughout the night the crew had to continually pump and bail out the vessel while severely frost bitten. Most of the oil was lost overboard and about 200 quintals of the fish was badly damaged. At daylight, the next morning, the exhausted crew were able to head back to land when the wind changed to westward and moderated. At 10 o'clock, they made Cape Race and then headed back to St. John's. They arrived Friday much to the relief of many people in St. John's because "much anxiety prevailed" for their safety.[15]

The author of the last account stated that few people in St. John's could recall witnessing such severe weather at that season of the year. But down through the years, there were many severe storms resulting in a great loss of people and ships. On February 10, 1817 a heavy gale from southwest continued for several hours wreaking havoc with the shipping in St. John's Harbour. Several vessels that were cutting out through the ice, broke from their moorings. The brigs *Maid of the Mill* drove out through the Narrows and to sea, the *Sidbury* went ashore at Maggoty Cove, the *James and Mary* struck on the Chain Rock and the *Caledonia* struck on the Pancake Shoal.[16]

[See Appendix 1 for more wind-related tragedies]

The Winter of the Rals 1817-1818

The port of St. John's was often isolated during harsh winter conditions. Some winters saw the waters frozen solid halting all shipping traffic for weeks on end. This was a potentially dangerous situation when food supplies were low and the only pipeline for relief was over the ocean and through the Narrows. The winter of 1817-1818 was one of the coldest in Newfoundland and was referred to as the 'Winter of the Rals' or rowdies because of the many riots which took place.

On November 11, 1817, there was a major fire in St. John's causing much destruction in loss of houses and food supplies. Two weeks later there was another fire on November 25. By the time word got out and relief was organized to be sent to the sufferers, the weather had turned very cold and the harbour started to freeze over.

After the fires and frost came famine where half the population lived off the other half with neither faring very well. In the depth of all this misery, the anxious citizens of St. John's looked out the harbour one day and saw an American ship coming through the ice! Since it was just four years after the American war, the people considered it a generous gesture of friendship.

Fortunately, the brig *Messenger* got in with relief supplies from Boston before traffic was brought to a standstill. By February, 1818, the harbour was frozen over below Chain Rock halting all shipping traffic in and out of the town. Gangs of men were then employed to cut a channel through the ice to allow the *Messenger* to get free on February 8th.[17]

On March 3, 1818, the harbour and Narrows were ringing again with the sounds of men and ice-cutting tools as great exertions were made to cut a channel through the ice which by now was 3 to 4 feet thick., Captain Baldwin was waiting anxiously to sail to England to take the body of Governor Francis Pickmore back home in the H.M.S. *Fly*. His Excellency, aged 62, had died a week before. His body was removed from government house and placed in a vault in the church with much ceremony. Admiral Pickmore was the first resident governor of the then colony of Newfoundland and the only one to die in office. He had come at a very bad time in the history of St. John's because there had been several disastrous fires, the price of fish had fallen very low resulting in mass starvation and outbreaks of violence.The winter must have been very severe because it took three weeks to cut a channel through the ice to get the ship out the Narrows..

Early March was also the time for the annual sailing of the seal fishery fleet but they were very late in sailing that year;

> "The early part of last week afforded a truly interesting scene, and anxious bustle in this Harbour, from a general effort, we may say, of the people in this community to get the Sealers to sea. They have been detained so long with contrary winds, and an ice-bound coast, that great fears began to be entertained as to the probability of their getting clear before the season was too far advanced......"[18]

Imagine the noise of sails flapping , men shouting , horns blaring as the 95 sailing vessels carrying 2040 men finally left to hunt the seals late in March,1818. All the schooners cleared the Narrows safely and headed North to the iceflows.

Cutting a channel through the ice in St. John's Harbour, c., 1850 (CNS)

The Royal Gazette has issues missing from April 14, 1818 to December 1827. So the next four accounts were taken from *The Mercantile Journal*;

> [November 17,1825] "The Schooner *Hope*, Wm. McGregor, Master, from Lunenburg, in working through the Narrows, on Tuesday last, missed stays and ran against the rocks on the north side. Signals of distress were immediately made, and the boats of H.M.S. *Grasshopper*, and those of His Excellency's Yacht, (the *Forte*) were sent to her assistance - and with the timed efforts of several others from shore, she was happily brought into port, having sustained but trifling damage. We have often before had to remark the ready attention which is given to signals of distress from his Majesty's ships, lying in this port. The exertions of Lieut. Langrishe, of H.M.S. *Grasshopper*, and Mr. Cooper, of the *Forte*, on this occasion was truly praiseworthy."

> [February 2,1826] "The Schr., *Ranger*, of Quebec, Armstrong, Master, was driven from her anchorage on Monday morning last, the wind blowing

strong from the W.N.W., and stranded between Chain Rock and the shore; where she remained during the day, but was got off about two o'clock on the following morning, and towed in abreast of Messrs. J. Dunscomb & Co.'s wharf. From the injury she had received it was found impractable to keep her free, having in a short time become completely water-logged. She had about 400 qtls. Of fish on board at the time of the accident, the greater part of which had been saved."

[March 16,1826] "Yesterday an Inquest was held on the body of Corporal Sharp of the Royal Artillery. On the previous evening, Sharp in company with a Mr. Graham, School-master, was attempting to go to the South Side, when the former fell through the Ice and was unfortunately drowned. - He has left a wife and four children. Graham suffered much from the cold; when discovered he was clinging to a post under one of the stages at the South Side, quite insensible."

[February 15,1827] "The Brig *Jackson*, belonging to Messrs. *Gosse, Pack & Fryer*, of Carbonear, *Howe,* Master, reached the Narrows on Tuesday last, From *Demerara*, after a severe passage of 49 days. She first made her appearance off Cape Spear, on Sunday evening last, with the wind about west, but blowing so hard that she could not make sail, consequently on the following morning she had drifted a considerable distance to the Northward of this port; about noon she was boarded by the pilots, whose perservance on this occasion is truly commendable; and the united efforts of the two crews, succeeded in the course of that day and night in beating her up into St. John's Bay, and on the Tuesday morning anchored her safe in the Narrows. The Jackson got soundings on the banks, 19 days before she reached this port. The crew's sufferings have been very great, one of which died, and we understand it was the Captain's intention, had he not received assistance that day and the weather continued so severe, to bear up."

The HMS Tyne

Besides winds and ice, the fogs around Newfoundland's coast gave the seafarers a lot of anxious moments. Sometimes it was only the good seamanship and fearlessness of the crew and captain that saved a vessel. Captain Sir. R. Grant of His Majesty's Ship *Tyne* was one of these determined, brave seaman. On Thursday, July 30, 1829, he left Harbour Grace after completing a northern cruise in the king's service. En route to St. John's, the ship encountered a foul wind with thick fog. Unable to enter the Narrows, the ship repeatedly fired her guns to alert lookouts on shore. Although the ship was in sight of Signal Hill for more than an hour when the fog partially cleared up, she was not noticed by the men at the signal-post there nor were the guns returned as usual from Fort Amherst. This neglect however, did not deter Sir. R. Grant from his course as he was determined to get into St. John's Harbour. Calling upon his seafaring knowledge and skill, he ordered his crew to fire the ship's guns repeatedly and listened to the echoes off the cliffs. Steering towards the directions from when the echo emanated, the ship entered safely into the Narrows before the signal for a Man-of-War was made at Signal Hill. *The Royal Gazette* said they were not used to laud officers who are supposed to have a knowledge of the harbours and coastline of this station. However, they must have been very impressed with Captain Grant for they praised him for his "cool and determined exhibition of his great abilities as a Naval Officer".[19]

On Monday, the *Tyne* was a pretty sight in St. John's Harbour as she was "superbly decorated in colours and flags", to celebrate the occasion of the marriage of Lieut. Smyth Griffith to Miss Green. Perhaps that had been an added incentive for their daring dash through the foggy Narrows a few days earlier!

After the incident with the *Tyne*, in 1829, the Captain must have complained to the local authorities about Fort Amherst, however, the following compliment was given Fort Amherst and the Governor in the July 6, 1830 edition of *The Royal Gazette*;

> "The firing of the fog guns at Fort Amherst as directed by His Excellency the Governor, has, we are informed, been of great service to vessels approaching the land in thick weather. We have heard many ship-masters state, that they have been almost solely enabled to make the harbour in consequence of this salutary measure - and for this fresh instance of His Excellency's attention to the welfare of the trade, we conceive the thanks of the community to be particularly due."

A month after the *Tyne's* triumphant victory against the elements a much smaller craft had a tragic experience in the Narrows. Early in September, 1829 between the hours of 8 and 9, Monday evening, Mr. John Angell and three companions were returning in a boat after mooring a schooner owned by Mr.Chafe, in Petty Harbour. The night was very dark and the wind was blowing "excessively strong" when the boat struck upon Anchor Rock (Pancake Rock). The boat instantly turned over and all four men were thrown out. Fortunately for three of them, they landed on the rock but Angell was drowned. A boat following them rescued the stranded men and they all managed to recover Angell's body immediately. Even though they tried in every way to revive him, "the vital spark had fled". John Angell, 28 years old, was the son of Mr. Edward Angell a resident of St. John's. The young man's remains were interred at Petty Harbour.[20]

There were far too many tragedies and incidents that happened just outside St. John's Bay to relate in one book. However the following account shows the uncertainty of the seafaring life. On April 9 1830, the brig *William & Ann* sunk in heavy ice just east of St. John's. Captain Parry and crew saved themselves by climbing onto the ice and were picked up by a fishing schooner bound for New York. They had no choice but to continue to New York even through they were so close to their destination. They later returned to St. John's from New York aboard another vessel.[21]

Terror from the Sky

St. John's, and the neighbouring communities in Freshwater Bay and Blackhead Bay were busy fishing centers in the 1800s. With the large number of fishing boats and fishermen on the local grounds, there was bound to be accidents. A very sad accident occurred on July 4, 1831, on the fishing ground near Cape Spear. On Monday morning a heavy thunder storm accompanied with very vivid lightning and torrents of rain arose between 7 and 8 o'clock. William Mulloy, his father and Mr. Moore were anchored on the fishing ground when they noticed the storm coming. Each sought shelter in the boat; Mulloy crawled into the fore-cubby while his father got into the after-cubby. Suddenly, a bolt of lightning struck the foremast splitting it nearly from top to bottom and sending it crashing down where the younger Mulloy was lying down. Moore, still seeking protection, discovered poor Mulloy expiring from the blow. An inquest was later held on the death, "the Jury therefore returned a verdict in accordance with these facts."[22]

The same storm was creating terror for a family up on Signal Hill. The flag-staff on the Block House was struck by lightning and rent to pieces sending splinters flying a fair distance. The "electric fluid" entered the building tearing a door off its hinges, continued on into a room where there were several children. One of the children was slightly injured but the dog lying under the table was killed. After doing some other minor damage, the lightning passed out at the side of the house.

The unpredictable winds off the harbour's entrance caused this tragic accident in August, 1842;

> "Melancholy Accident. - On Monday evening last a fishing boat belonging to Mr. Francis Shepherd of Harbor Grace, was proceeding on her way to the Westward, when nearly off the entrance of this harbor a sudden squall of wind upset her, and we regret to say that Mr. Shepherd's two sons and a man named Shoot were unfortunately drowned, the later leaving a wife and eight helpless children in the greatest poverty and distress. - Shoot had a son in the boat with him at the time of the accident, but he most fortunately seized an oar, and another boat coming to his assistance he was rescued from a watery grave."[23]

The ice was so tight to shore on April 2, 1846, that two harbour pilots, William Vinnecombe and James Cantwell stepped off the North Head of the Narrows and clambered over the ice pans to the *William Warren* lying about 5 miles off the port. They left 2 o'clock in the afternoon and when they reached the vessel 1 ½ hours later, they informed the master, James Carroll that there were lots of seals within 3/4 of a mile of the vessel. The men were immediately sent off to kill and sculp (skin) the seals; one man was seen from the vessel's deck killing up to 100 seals in a short space of time. The pilots on returning, reported the seals to be in great numbers off St. John's and the ice to be very rough. The paper praised the pilots for their journey, " for the danger was very great".[24]

The Gale of '46

On Saturday, September 19, 1846, one of the most terrible and destructive gales of wind and rain that ever visited Newfoundland to that time, occurred. It would be known for many generations after as the gale of 1846. Early in the afternoon a wind was blowing from the northeast accompanied by incessant torrents of rain. The wind gradually veered to the northward, increasing in intensity until at 4 p.m. it was blowing a violent gale. The rain abated in the evening but the wind continued to blow at a terrifying rate during the night only subsiding towards morning. The wind storm wreaked havoc all over Newfoundland destroying much property and taking many lives. In St. John's, the Native's Hall was blown down killing a 5 year old boy Duggan and his 20 year old sister. The hall has been a temporary shelter to several families who had been displaced by a terrible fire earlier on the ninth of June. St. Thomas Church was shifted several inches off its foundation and in the harbour several ships were damaged and some sunk. Two tragedies occurred in and near the Narrows. A fishing boat with seven men aboard was trying to gain the inner harbour when it was swamped in the Narrows and all the occupants perished. Another vessel owned by Mr. Coyell of St. John's was trying to get in with a load of fish and oil from Twillingate. Unable to make the harbour, the vessel was driven ashore in Freshwater Bay, went to pieces and one of the crew was drowned. For weeks after, news trickled in from all over the island of death and destruction from the gale of 1846.[25]

The Wreck of the Avalon

On Tuesday night, February 1, 1848, a terrible shipwreck occurred right at the entrance to the harbour. The brigantine *Avalon* belonging to Mr. William Walsh of St. John's, had arrived early Tuesday morning from Glasgow with a cargo of coal. The Narrows was blocked up with ice so the *Avalon* was anchored a short distance from the southern head to wait a chance to get in through the ice. She was there all day and at 11 o'clock that night a strong wind sprang up from east north east and grew in strength until midnight. The crew and captain struggled valiantly to save the ship from going on the rocks. People on shore were also assisting them but all in vain. The ill-fated ship was dashed against the rocks directly under the South Battery (Fort Amherst lighthouse). She fell on the rocks amidships and instantly went to pieces. Five of the crew of ten had climbed onto the jibboom and rigging for safety and when the ship struck and broke asunder, they were "ushered into eternity". Only the captain and four of his men escaped the awful disaster. The men who died were Patrick Walsh, 18, owner's son, Michael Hally, Patrick Condon, James Kelly and John McDonald. The article went on to say that, "the calamity seems enhanced by the reflection that it occurred under the eye of the shore and still it was impossible to have rendered effectual and timely assistance, such were the violence of the storm, the darkness of the night and the shortness of the time that elapsed after the vessel first struck until the work of destruction and death was completed."[26]

Later that same Spring, another shipwreck took place on the opposite side of the Narrows near Wash Pots or Wash Balls, partly submerged rocks immediately off the North Head.

> "Early on Friday evening last, the schr. *Commix*, Philip Walsh, master, from Placentia Bay, with 400 lbs. Herrings on board, in coming into the harbour misstayed, and on attempting to wear her she was drawn towards the Wash Pots; they dropped anchor, but she drove against the rocks, and on striking parted and sunk, the crew barely having time to escape by lowering themselves by a rope from the main boom into the Pilot boat (No.1) of John Vinicombe."[27]

The two shipwrecks in 1848 must have gotten the local authorities thinking about safety in the Narrows and approaches. In the October 3, 1848 edition of *The Royal Gazette*, the public was informed;

> "The Times states that the materials for the construction of a life-boat, to be kept at Fort Amherst, have been received at the Ordnance Department here."

A year later, in August 1849, the Royal Artillery in Newfoundland were supplied with a rescue devise invented by Captain Manby. Manby's Apparatus was kept at Fort Amherst on the South Side to afford assistance in case of shipwreck, "to prevent such loss of life as occurred last year close to the harbour".[28]

In 1845, the pilots had petitioned the government for a steam tug at the entrance of the harbour to tow vessels in. Efforts were being made to make the hazardous Narrows less dangerous.

A schooner passes very near the Southern Head of the Narrows (City of St. John's Archives)

Sail and Steam

In the mid 1800s, steamships were starting to replace sailing vessels. The first steamship that entered the Narrows was the H.M.S. *Spitfire*, on November 5, 1840. By 1854, St. John's was being considered as a port of call for the steamers of the Collins Line which ran between New York and Liverpool. On Saturday, April 22,1854, the steamer, *Victoria* arrived with a naval surveyor to examine St. John's harbour. The surveyor was satisfied with the harbour except for a sunken rock on the south side of the Narrows. The Governor immediately assented to grant the sum of £400 for the removal of the rock. The port of St. John's would now see more steamers entering port which would eventually spell the demise of the age of sail. These steamers would get bigger and bigger and require more space (water depth) to safely enter the Narrows.

Sailing directions for the island of Newfoundland written in 1851, told vessels how to approach and enter the harbour of St. John's and the rocks to avoid. These instructions could also benefit steamers;

".......There are three bays between Cape Spear and the entrance to St. John's: 1, Cape Bay lying between Cape Spear and Black Head; 2, Deadman's Bay between Black Head and Small Point; and 3, Freshwater Bay between Small Point and Fort Amherst.

From Fort Amherst, on the south head at the entrance of St. John's Harbour, there is shown a brilliant fixed light, which, from its elevation, may be seen at a considerable distance. ST. JOHN'S HARBOUR......Fort Amherst, on its south side, or point of entrance. The channel, from point to point is only about one-sixth of a mile wide; but it gets wider as you approach the Chain Rock; for, from the latter to Pancake Rock, the distance is only 95 fathoms, these rocks being above water and steep-to: Chain is the northern rock, and Pancake Rock lies on the south side of the channel. Three small knolls lie between the two latter rocks in the narrows, with 18 to 24 feet on them.

In approaching the harbour....avoid the Vestal Rock, which lies about 50 fathoms off the southern or Fort Amherst Point; over this rock are 18 feet water....the course is N.W. by W., the shore continuing bold until you get near to the Pancake, then give the south side a small berth; continue the same course or rather more inclined to the westward, keeping Fort Amherst flagstaff open to the northward of Frederick's Battery flag-staff; you will, by these means avoid the Prosser, a rock on the port side, running off the end of another rock, formed like a saddle with 18 feet water in the hollow, and only 5 feet on its outside; yet it is steep-to, having not less that 5 fathoms close to it; so soon as you are within, you have passed the Prosser Rock, you may steer up as you please.....

The winds....either baffle or blow out the Narrows....you must warp in for the convenience of doing which rings are fixed in the rocks on either side.......

.....be careful nor to mistake Kitty Vitty....while St. John's Harbour may be distinguished by Fort Amherst, which appears white........"[29]

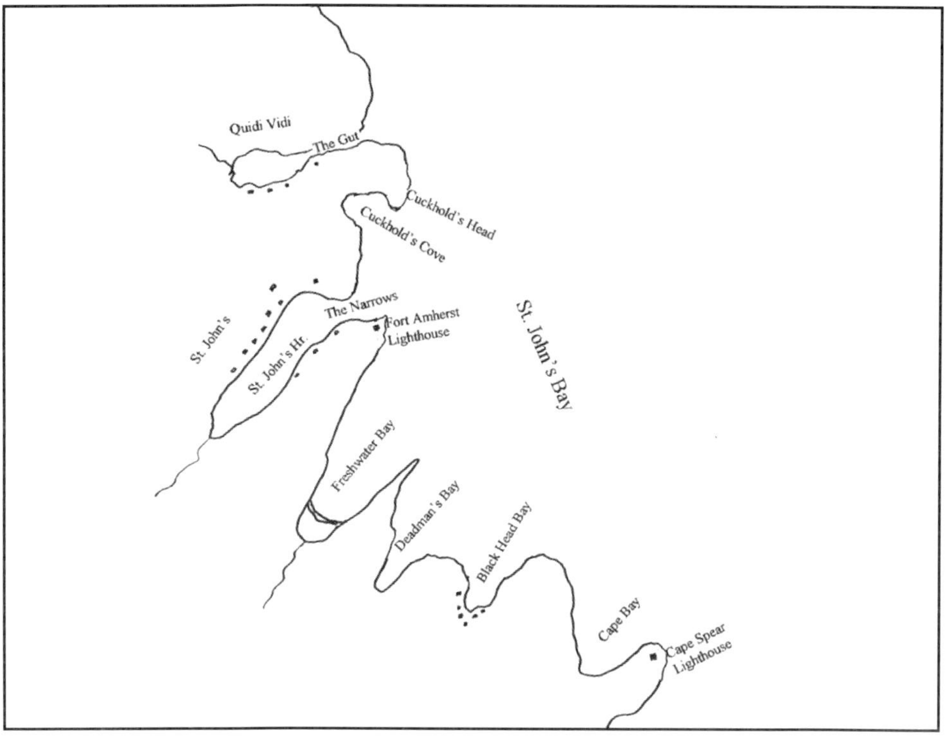

St. John's Bay showing headlands and bays (Author)

A Heroic Rescue at the South Battery

There were still plenty of sailing vessels using the port of St. John's when the 1851 sailing directions were penned. Unfortunately, there were also more accidents such as the one which happened right under the Fort Amherst light station in May, 1854. Here is the thrilling story of the heroic rescue;

> "The following act of faithful and effective perseverance should not be passed over without public approbation and a suitable reward.
>
> It appears that about ½ past 3 o'clock on the morning of Thursday week, the men at Fort Amherst were alarmed by the report of a small gun, when they immediately hurried out, and then heard a fearful cry as though of men in the utmost distress and on hailing them through the speaking trumpet, their reply was that they were sinking, and implored instant succor to save their lives. Sergeant Oxley, R.N.C. then fired two alarm guns, in the hope of arousing the people in a Schooner lying there, but the cry that they were sinking continuing, four of the

men at the Fort immediately procured their own boat which was about three-quarters of a mile distant, and proceeded out the narrows, hailing three vessels as they went but without getting an answer from any of them.On reaching the vessel in distress, they ascertained there were nine men on board, the soldiers found they could not take them all off at once, as it was then blowing a gale,- the master of the vessel urged them to take off as many as they could and pass them in safety, and come off for the rest as they could not keep their craft afloat much longer. The rescue party took out three of them one of whom had broken his ribs when their Boat struck, and having put them on board another Western Boat being in the Narrows, and got three hands from her, they went our again to the vessel, which appeared nearly in a sinking condition, and having got the pump and bucket from the other boat, and further assistance from the *Iron Duke*, they continued pumping, and succeeded in keeping the vessel sufficiently free until the crew of the *Iron Duke* brought her into the wharf of Messrs. Job & Co., at the Southside, at about 7 o'clock.

The craft saved was a Western Deck Boat from Perlican and Island Cove, coming round here for supplies, and the names of those humane and heroic rescuers are Corporal, *John Humphreys,* Privates, *William Downey, John Taylor*, and *Robert Ward.* We sincerely trust that proper means will be adopted to raise a testimonial to these men for their services, and as an encouragement to others under similar circumstances."[30]

More Improvements for Shipping

While the sailing vessels and small fishing crafts had a difficult time trying to avoid the rocks on both sides of the Narrows, they could easily glide over the Merlin and Ruby Rocks, two submerged rocks right in the middle of the channel. The Ruby Rock was between the Chain Rock and the Little Pancake while the Merlin Rock was further in and to the left of Ruby. Larger steam ships drawing more water, were frequenting the port and the Merlin Rock especially was becoming a hazard. Therefore, work was begun in the summer of 1855 to remove this hazard or at least, reduce it. By mid August, the work was nearly completed as described in this report;

"The destruction of the Merlin Rock it is expected will be accomplished in two more days. The east and west sides have been removed, leaving a ridge or back bone extending in a north and south direction, about 20 feet in length and 6 in breath still to be broken. The fragments fall into a depth of 60 feet round the rock, a mere trifle only remaining on the top, which is removed by means of a drag, made of iron, with edge serrated. The depth of water to be obtained is 27 feet, not 23 as previously stated. - This is depth sufficient to admit the *Persia*, the largest steamer now afloat, which, with engines on board and fully laden, draws 23 feet water, her burden being 3,000 tons in excess of the largest Cunard steamer now running. It is much to be desired that the Government will authorize the removal of the obstruction at the entrance of Quidi Vidi, which would facilitate a vastly more successful prosecution of the fishery from that place."[31]

When the contractors, Messrs. Husted & Krochi had the Merlin blasted away to a depth of 27 feet below the low water mark, they had to return again to blast away a quantity of rock which had settled upon the top of the Merlin instead of sinking in the depths beside it. However, due to time and weather restrictions, they decided to engage the diver from the Flag-ship H.M.S. *Boscawen* to go down and push the ruble off manually. The Flag-ship later passed over the spot where the Merlin Rock had been. These rocks would be the subject of more blasting in the near future.

[See Appendix 5 For more information about these rocks]

In May of 1857, a chart of the St. John's harbour was completed and to further aid shipping, it was proposed to place a bell on Cape Spear. In foggy weather, the light there was of no use to ships at sea. Apparently, the steam-ship *Khersonee* had barely avoided a collision with the cape on her last trip to St. John's when she passed so close by the cape that the sound of her propeller and the voices on deck was distinctly heard by the light keeper there. But the biggest forward step taken in 1857 to aid shipping in and out of the port was the acquisition of a steam-tug in September;

"On Wednesday night the *Dauntless*, a fine new Clyde built tug-boat, owned by David Steele, Esq., arrived here, in 17 days from Swansea. She is intended for this port, and will supply a want long much felt. The *Dauntless* is a paddle-boat, 80 feet long, 76 tons builders' measurement, 40 horse power but will work up to 65. She was launched last fall, and its to be commanded by Captain Taylor, later of the *James Stewart*. We are satisfied she will prove as remunerative to her enterprising owner as she will be serviceable to the trade."[32]

Looking out through the Narrows from St. John's, c., 1850 (CNS)

The Dauntless Earns Her Pay

An advertisement was placed in *The Royal Gazette* on September 15, 1857, by David Steele announcing the rates of towage and distance the tug was willing to go, etc., and stating that the boat did not intend to ply on Sundays. Vessels anchored in the Narrows on that day would be attended to the first on Monday morning. Also, stated was that, "vessels in distress or otherwise disabled would have to make *special* contracts for assistance."

How would a vessel sinking in a storm or someone drowning be able to enter into a special contract to save them immediately ? Did the *Roderick Random* have a chance to do so? Abutting the tug boat ad was the account of an accident to the schooner. Two days earlier, on Saturday, the *Roderick Random* was sailing out the Narrows when she ran into an incoming boat from Catalina laden with fish. The six or seven people in the boat were hurled into the water and struggled there until the Pilot boat rescued them. Unfortunately, one of them, a woman lost her life.[33]

However, the *Dauntless* would prove her worth over the years. A month after the September ad appeared in the papers, the steam-tug proved very useful to the schooner *Billow.* The *Billow* was heading out the Narrows bound for Burin, when she ran on the rocks at Hay Cove. The schooner would have gone to pieces but for the quick action of the tug which came to the rescue and towed the schooner off the shore. The *Billow* was considerably damaged but no lives were lost and the vessel was saved.[34]

Less than a year later, the *Dauntless* felt what it was like to be the rescued instead of the rescuer when it was wrecked on the infamous Cahill's or Prosser's Rock. In an article in *The Evening Telegram*, April 1, 1920, H.F. Shortis gave all the details of the wreck;

> "On this date, 1858, the tug-boat Dauntless was engaged in towing the brip Spray, Capt. Roper.......The Spray was bound for Pernambuco, Brazil, with a cargo of codfish.....The wind was blowing a storm at the time from the North East, with a heavy sea; and Cape Spear grounds, Old Hamen and Old Harry breaking "mountainous high". When about one mile outside the Narrows, the Dauntless let go the Spray, and was returning to St. John's. Coming through the Narrows, the Dauntless, Capt. Mearns, to show the passengers on board, who were friends of Capt. Roper, the scenery, kept too near Cahill's Rock on the South Side and she struck the rock, smashing her bottom and sinking in a short time. Boats from the shore, which witnessed the accident, hurried to the assistance....... and succeeded in rescuing the entire company......C.F. Bennett & Co. Purchased the sunken steamer, and, after a short time, an arrangement was entered into with the famous master-builder, Michael Kearney, who succeeded in raising her on the 24th July of the same year. The manner in which he carried out the operations was.....He procured two foreign-going vessels.....and with very large spars, lashed together with chains from one vessel to the other, one against the foremast and one against the mainmast, across the vessel, he started the undertaking. Kearney placed the two vessels on either side, above the sunken tug-boat, and then sent down the diver to "sweep her", by placing chains under her bottom, one forward and the other aft. When this was done satisfactorily, he filled the two ships with water, at low tide, and secured the chain "frapes" that were around the tug-boat. He then got the ships pumped out, and as the tide rose, it lifted the tug-boat and she was brought in shoaler water..."

The author continued by describing in detail how they repeated the process and got the tug up to the surface and how they got got her onto Mudge's Dock on the South Side to repair her. He included one verse of a poem written by "the poet of Pokeham Path, Power", who wrote about the sinking of the Dauntless;

> "T'was on the 1st of April, in the middle of the day,
> The Dauntless went down the Harbor to tow out McBride's Spray;
> She towed her to the Southern Head, and quickly cast her off,
> And on her way returning she struck on Cahill's Rock.
> She struck on Cahill's Rock, my boys, and tore away her keel,
> And down went the old Dauntless belonging to Davy Steele.
> Mearns, he was the captain, Dick Roche was second hand,
> And all the rest of the jolly crew belonged to Newfoundland;
> And as I went down on the wharf, it was to my surprise,
> To see the gallant Davy Steele with tears all in his eyes."[35]

The Royal Gazette on April 6, 1858 added that the *Dauntless* was returning by the same route she always took. But because of a heavy swell on at the time, the bow struck the rock and she passed over the rock her full length before going down in less than four minutes. She was going at full speed when she struck. There wasn't much time for the people on board to save themselves as they scrambled into the steamer's boat while some jumped overboard. The engineer went down with the vessel but was recovered by the others and became very ill. Boats from the shore immediately came out to rescue the shipwrecked folks.

By January, the next year, the Dauntless was again in service on the waters around St. John's. Her final fate was to be wrecked at Dildo on September 10, 1877.

The steam tug was probably engaged to search for three boys who drowned off the Fort Amherst light house in April, 1859;

> "DISTRESSING OCCURRENCE. - On Saturday afternoon, three boys, named HARVEY, TAYLOR AND KOUGH, sons of respectable parents on the South Side, went down as far (as) Fort Amherst, and when last seen were amusing themselves about the rocks there, since which they have been missing, and it is feared that they must have slid off into the sea and been washed away by the surf."[36]

Schooner at left in Gunner's Cove just after passing Cahill's Rock (MHA)

A Royal Visit and a Grand Accolade

During the summer of 1860, St. John's was host to His Royal Highness, the Prince of Wales, the future King Edward VII, oldest son of Queen Victoria. He arrived in the 91 gun ship *Hero* on July 23rd accompanied by the ships *Ariadne* and *Flying Fish.* The royal visit wasn't expected until the next day. However, as if by magic, flags, banners, streamers and mottoes were displayed as soon as the three ships entered the Narrows. A royal salute was given from the Queen's Battery as the bells of the Roman Catholic Cathedral pealed forth followed by the bells of various other churches in the city. An air of excitement ran through the city as people streamed to the waterfront to catch a glimpse of the royal party. After a three-day whirlwind tour of the city the royal party left on July 26th amid much fanfare.

A month before the royal visit, buoys had been placed in the Narrows, one over Ruby Rock and another on the outer edge of the Pancake. Before they were laid, the *Niagara* had struck the Ruby Rock. When the *Hero* left with the royal party both the Ruby and Merlin Rocks were detonated to explode. The ships got underway around eleven o'clock in the morning and steamed slowly out the Narrows, the *Ariadne* leading, followed by the *Hero* and *Flying Fish.* The steam-tug *Dauntless*, decorated from stem to stern with flags and carrying No. 1 Company of Rifles, accompanied the Prince's entourage along with a flotilla of crafts. Throngs of people cheered, cannons from the batteries and ships boomed. By the Chain Rock Battery, a large crowd had gathered; the Prince bowed gallantly as the ladies waved their handkerchiefs to him and everyone sang "God Save the Queen" as they went by. Then as the *Hero* passed through the Narrows, the blasts on the submerged rocks were discharged with loud explosions, throwing up water on either side in foam high above the ship's decks.[37] It was a most memorable occasion for all concerned; a much happier event than the usual shipwrecks and groundings which took place annually in the Narrows.

His Royal Highness must have been impressed with the scenic beauty of the Narrows and harbour of St. John's and the enthusiastic send-off he was given. An earlier visitor, Mr. Church had been so impressed with his visit to Newfoundland in 1859 that he wrote a book about it and said this about the entrance;

"The harbor of St. John's is certainly one of the most remarkable for bold and effective scenery on the Atlantic shore. The pictures of it, which of late abound, and are quite truthful as miniature portraits, fail entirely to suggest the grand expression and strong character of the coast. We were moving spiritedly forward over a bright and lively sea, watching the stern head lands receding in the South and starting out to view in the North, while we passed Cape Spear, a lofty promontory, crowned with a light house and signal shaft, upon which was floating the meteor-flag of England, and at once found ourselves abreast the bay in front of St. John's. Not a vestige though of anything like a city was in sight except another flag floating on a distant pinnacle of rock. Like a mighty Colliseum, the sea-wall half encircled the deep water of this outer bay, into which the full power of the ocean let itself under every wind except the westerly. Right towards the coast where it gathered itself up into the greatest massiveness, and tied itself up into a very Gordian knot, we cut across, curious to behold when and where the rugged adamant was going to split and let us through.At length it opened and we looked through, and presently glided through a kind of mountain pass. Around us and close above us, the rugged brown cliffs rose to a fine height, armed at certain points with cannon, and before us, to all appearance, opened out a most beautiful mountain lake, with a little city looking down from a mountain side, and a swarm of shipping along its shores. We were in the harbor and before St. John's. As we bade adieu to the sea, and hailed the land with our plucky little gun, the echoes rolled among the hills and rattled along the ricky galleries of the mountains in the finest style. We were quite delighted. So fresh and novel was the prospect, so unexpected were the peculiar sentiment and character of the scene, one could barely realize that it was old to the experience of tens of thousands. I could scarcely help feeling there was stupidity somewhere, that more had not been said about what had been seen by so many for so long a time........"[38]

The Christina: A Sealing Incident in Freshwater Bay

In the 1850s and 1860s the sealing fleet was at the zenith of its glory with regards to the quality of the vessels employed and the reputation of the master. Every March dozens of schooners would leave the port of St. John's and head north to the ice floes. The time of departure was a gala event;

"It was a grand sight yesterday to see our little sealing fleet taking advantage of the favorable change of wind, pressing out through the ice-bound gates of the narrows to the clear water beyond. Foremost of the fleet from early morning was our friend Capt. HALLERAN, in his *Livingstone*. Obstacles but seemed to give him and his crew fresh energy, and in the afternoon their efforts were crowned with success, for then the *Livingstone* burst her way into the blue water, and, with every stitch of canvas drawing, she sped round the northern head as though she had some especial business to attend to and was in a hurry to get through with it. She was followed soon after by Mr. MARCH'S *Corsair*. We believe these were the only two to get clear last evening, though others were at the edge of the ice at dark.........."[39]

The ice was very heavy that year and three weeks later the harbour was still in a "pitiable plight", blocked with ice as far as the eye could see seaward. The seal fishery was a disaster, and many ships were lost. The *Livingstone* returned on April 22, 1962 with no seals, the *Margaret,* Cummins master and the *Roxana*, Jackman master were only two of many vessels lost at sea that year. Up to April 16th, there were 20 sealers reported lost. The big story around St. John's that year was the suspected deliberate burning of the schooner *Christina* just outside the Narrows near Freshwater and Blackhead Bays. Local papers were full of conflicting stories from Captain Parsons of the *Christina* and John Walsh from Blackhead about the destruction of the vessel.

The *Christina* was a 142 ton schooner with a crew of 54 men. She was supplied by Punton & Munn of Harbor Grace for the 1862 seal fishery. Around 7 o'clock on Saturday, April 5th she was abandoned and burned while in a sinking condition, stuck in the ice off St. John's. Word got about that the *Christina* was deliberately set ablaze by her own crew. Questions were being asked in St. John's as to why weren't the riggings, sails, provisions, etc., first removed before the vessel was set afire. Captain Parsons accused the people of Blackhead and Freshwater Bay of plundering the vessel and setting her on fire before the captain had time to remove the valuables off the vessel. He denied that he or any of his crew did the deed. On April 11th, John Walsh went to the office of the Day-Book and gave his side of the story. The following is Walsh's statement to the *Day-Book*, April 12, 1862;

"The *Christina* was off Blackhead, from Thursday evening. On Saturday evening she had two topsails set, and had her head to the Southward, trying to get around the Cape. About half-past 5 o'clock in the evening I, with three others, went off and boarded her. When we got on board we found three Blackhead men there.They were tying up some provisions, and when they had them tied up they went ashore. There were then only four of the crew and the Captain aboard. I went down the main hatch, and began to cut some waste canvas which was lying about, and which had been cut before. I wanted the canvas to tie up some provisions in.

> While engaged in doing this I heard the Captain singing out from the deck, ordering all hands up from below. He said he couldn't allow such work to be carried on. That was the first time I heard or saw anything of the Captain. We then dropped everything and went on deck. I spoke to the Captain, and told him the vessel was in a sinking condition, and he might as well let the poor people get something out of her as have it go down with her. The Captain said, "I can't see things destroyed in that form." I knew the vessel would soon go down, unless active exertions were made to keep her afloat, and then there was nobody on board to do it. So, on my own responsibility, I went below again by myself. When I got below I saw a man in the cabin, whom I believe to be a master of watch. I asked him where the bread was. He showed me where it was, and stood by me while I was getting it. At this time the Captain was on deck...........I went on deck and spoke to the Captain. I told him there was plenty of Pork and Flour down there, and it was a pity to have it lost.....He told me I might go down and take a barrel of flour......I told the Captain six or seven Freshwater men were coming............Presently the Freshwater men raised the hatches and went below......I went below again......at this time there was not more than two feet of water in the vessel.....one of the men on deck...sung out to me,"John Walsh, Come up- they're going to sot her afire."....I put the candle out and went on deck. When I got up I said to the Captain, "Captain, what time did the vessel begin to make water?" He replied, "About 8 o'clock this morning." I then said, "Did you try the pumps?" He said, "No, I did not- there's no use in trying the pumps". ....I saw smoke coming up from the fore scuttle, the Captain then standing at the gangway. He said to me, "She's afire." I said, "It's a pity she should be afire." He replied, "It is a pity." Knowing that I had put the candle out, I said to him, "Perhaps it was the candle that was down below had set fire to some shavings." He said, turning away with a smile, "Perhaps it was."...........after I saw the smoke coming up out of the after hatch."

Everybody then left the ship, the captain and three crewmen headed for the city while Walsh left for Blackhead. He had extended an invitation to Captain Parsons to come to his place for the night which was refused. As they were all leaving, someone mentioned the powder in the vessel which hastened everyone's steps over the ice. Some of the crew from the *Christina* must have walked over the ice as far as the Fort Amherst light house because in the 1863 House of Assembly Journal, money was allocated for the, " expenses of 49 men at Fort Amherst". The schooner was still afloat the next morning so Walsh returned very early and saw that the vessel had burned down to 18 inches below the ice. By 7 o'clock in the morning, the ice was rafting over her. A few days later, the *Day-Book* ran an article in which they discredited Walsh's story and defended Captain Parsons' honor. No doubt, the *Christina* incident was discussed long after she disappeared below the ice in St. John's Bay.

Freshwater Bay with wrecked ship on beach (PANL)

A Harrowing Experience in the Gitana

On Christmas morning, 1862, St. John's was abuzz with the rumor that the *Gitana* was lost the night before just outside the Narrows. The *Gitana,* Captain Jackman, belonged to Messrs. J. B. Barnes & Co. and was ten days out from New York with a valuable cargo for its owners. Although the rumors proved to be untrue, the *Gitana* came extremely close to wrecking below Fort Amherst in an incident similar to the *Avalon* which had met destruction there 14 years previous. It was only through the superhuman exertions of the pilot, Mr. Charles Lewis, Captain Jackman and the crew that the vessel was saved and no lives were lost. Around 11:30 on Wednesday night, December 24th, Pilot Lewis boarded the *Gitana* a quarter of a mile off the Southern Head. By 1:00 a.m. she was safely anchored in the Narrows, sails furled, a watch set for the night, awaiting the tug expected early the next morning. There was no indication of bad weather. Another vessel, the *Volant* was anchored inside of her. However, at 4 a.m. a gale suddenly sprung up from the N.N.E. with a heavy sea breaking against the Southern Head. The *Gitana* began to drag her anchor and drifted in under the Southern Head so the ship's boat was lowered as a route of escape if they couldn't get her away. Pilot Lewis called over to the *Volant* to go get the tug and they replied that the pilot boat had gone for her. By now, the *Gitana* was broadside the rocks and the seas were breaking outside of her throwing her in against the cliff. Pilot Lewis shouted for the men to stand by to slip the chain. As the cable was slipped, four of the men who figured the vessel was doomed, jumped into the boat and shoved off. The pilot and the captain sang out to the "cowards" to come back and two of them did. Just as these would-be deserters got back on deck, the brig responded to the desperate efforts to clear the rocks. The jib was loosened and hoisted and the brig turned round towards the E.S.E. The two topsails were then put on her and with other sails being put on, she "cleared the Bay with her lee rail under water". However, she wasn't out of danger yet for by the time they got five miles outside of Cape Spear, it was blowing strongly from the N.N.E. with a big sea running and nasty snow-squalls. Things were only going from bad to worse as the dark stormy night at sea wore on. At 8:00 a.m. on Christmas morning, the pilot thought it would be best run for Bay Bulls but the captain figured it would be impossible to make the harbour in the driving snow and rough seas. Therefore, they hove to and by 4:00 p.m. the brig was abreast of Bay Bulls, 18 miles off heading N.W. The tired men were still a long ways from home. At daylight on Friday morning, Boxing Day, it was still blowing strong from the N.W. Bay Bulls was now 28 miles to the N.W. as they set all the sails and headed in. At 8:00 a.m. they got within 17 miles of the land which they thought was Cape Broyle. By dark that day they were 32 miles off Cape Spear with a wind from the S.E. The pilot then ran her and at 4:00 a.m. on Saturday they finally got to within 8 miles of the Cape Spear light. When the brig got to within 3 miles of the Cape, the tug *Dauntless* came alongside and wanted to tow her in. The Captain refused the service because, "when he was in danger and wanted her, he couldn't get her. Now that he was safe, and didn't want her, he could do without her." At 2:00 on Saturday, the pilot brought the *Gitana* into port with flying colors. They had battled and won against the wild seas and wind, the prize being their lives and the ship. During the ordeal, the pilot and captain had gone aloft with the crew to work in the riggings to save the brig. Everyone had reason to feel proud and relieved as they passed by the Southern Head where 4 days earlier death had stared them all in the face.[40]

Harbour Lights and More Controversy

In the spring of 1863, the harbour was being surveyed by Captain Orlebar in the surveying steamer *M. Stevenson.* A plan was being made of the St. John's harbour and leading lights were to be erected to aid steam ships entering at night. *The Royal Gazette* on May 26, 1863 wrote; " these leading lights will be of great importance, as the passage between the "Ruby" rock and the "Pancake" shoal, is only one hundred (100) yards wide."

In September, notices were placed in local papers announcing that two red lights would be exhibited every night as leading marks for vessels entering and leaving the Narrows. The local government was anxious to have the notice forwarded to different Atlantic Steam Companies as they anticipated more steam ships entering the port in the future. Two red lights were mounted to shine out the Narrows, one on the Custom House and the other near the Congregational Church.

Around the early part of December, some "miscreants" smashed out the light placed near the Congregational Church for the second time. A reward of fifty pounds was posted for information leading to the apprehension and conviction of the party or parties. It wasn't considered to be a boyish prank for the part destroyed was 3 inches thick requiring a hammer or something similar to smash it. Some papers hinted that the pilots or someone connected to them did it. On December 17th, *The Day-Book* ran two long articles defending the pilots calling them an "intelligent, respectable set of men, chosen after due examination to do an important duty, and one which necessarily calls for sobriety, intelligence and skill". Besides, there was no inducement for them to break out the light as foreign going vessels were obliged to take on a pilot whether required or not.

In 1873 a notice appeared in *The Royal Gazette* concerning the pilots of St. John's. Apparently, complaints had been made to the government about the apathy of the pilots in the discharge of their duties. At that time, the pilotage system consisted of several boats in competition with each other. Each boat had a master pilot and a crew of his own choosing, usually all family members such as the Ryan, Vinnicombe, Gallishaw and Lewis families. The apathy mentioned may have referred to the pilot boats refusing a cheap job in favor of a more lucrative one. The notice stated that on the next complaint being made to the Commissioners of Pilots, the negligent boat's crew will be suspended for a unspecified period of time. A month later in November, a long list of signals by which a ship in distress could signal for a pilot, was posted in *The Royal Gazette*.

However, in spite of the derogatory remarks about the pilots, they were very instrumental in many rescues in and around the Narrows down through the years. Theirs was a hazardous job performed in small boats and in all kinds of weather. Some pilots died an early death brought on by the rigors of his piloting lifestyle.

A brigantine in heavy seas (MHA)

The Arichat West

On Christmas Day, 1875, an incident occurred in the Narrows reminiscing of the *Gitano* struggle which had taken place there thirteen years earlier. Once again the Narrows was the scene of much anxiety and activity;

> "The Brigt. *Arichat West*, McDonald master, arrived and anchored at the mouth of the Narrows on the evening of the 25th, wind south and baffling. The night-boat on duty, in making her rounds of the Harbor, discovered a vessel in distress in the Narrows. On reaching the vessel, it was found to be the *Arichat West*. When the night-boat reached her she was nearly ashore on the North Head, but by the timely assistance rendered by the night-men, she was towed off. Capt. McDonald not liking his position sent on shore to advise the owner and to ask for the assistance of the *Dauntless,* which, however, could not be obtained, as she was laid up for the night; a couple of boats and some lines were sent out and preparation made for towing and warping the vessel in. Whilst getting underway a back flaw took the brigantine, causing her to strike the southern head, carrying away the rudder. She afterwards wheeled round and struck on the north side. At

daylight, the tug came to her assistance and towed her to the wharf of J. Woods, Esq., where she almost immediately sank. The *Arichat West* was owned we believe by J. Woods, Esq., also the cargo of 450 tons of Glace Bay coals with which she was laden. The wreck was sold yesterday at public auction for £150."[41]

The Mayaguezana Tragedy

On the night of August 14, 1876, a tragedy took place in Blackhead Bay that could have been avoided. The Spanish brig *Mayaguezana* was bound from Mayaguez, West Indies, to St. John's with a cargo of molasses and sugar. There was dense smoke on the waters approaching the Narrows from a fire in the woods upon the Southside Hills. The ship ran ashore at Blackhead and Captain Fioll, his wife 9 year old daughter and one crew member were drowned. One of the pilot boats brought in the rest of the crew. Two pilots were blamed for the disaster in this report to the Colonial Secretary by Judge Prowse on August 29th;

> "I have the honour to inform you that I have held a very protracted and searching enquiry into the cause of the death of Captain Fioll, master of the Spanish brigantine *Mayaguezana*, his wife and daughter on the night of the 14th August instant, and also as to the alleged neglect of the Pilots in not boarding the vessel on that evening. As there are charges against two pilot boats, Nos. 3 and 4, I will take them separately and commence with the charge against William Vinicombe, master of pilot boat No. 3. I find as the result of the enquiry, and established by the clearest evidence, that the said vessel, *Mayaguezana*, was off the mouth of the harbor from about 6 o'clock, on the evening of the 14th August, that she tacked at Cuckhold's Cove Head about 7 (just when the light was lit at Fort Amherst), and at a distance of less than half a mile from the mouth of the harbor; that she was seen by a great number of persons besides those whose evidence I have taken; that William Vinicombe himself saw her and must have been at times on that evening not more than a mile from her; that after Vinicombe had put Collins aboard the English schooner, *Queen of Clippers*, he had three hands in the boat, two of whom were pilots, that, the Spaniard being to leeward, he could easily have run down to her, and there was neither wind nor weather, nor any other obstacle to his putting a pilot aboard the Spanish vessel if he had chosen to do so; that, as he saw the Spaniard at the time he put Collins on Board the schooner, it was equally his duty to have given a pilot to the Spaniard as well as to the schooner; that, seeing she was a foreigner, night coming on, and there being so much smoke on the water, it was his imperative duty to have boarded her immediately after he boarded the schooner. As to Vinicombe's statement, and

the statements of the other pilots, that they could not find the Spanish vessel again after once seeing her, and that they did not know she was bound here, & c., they are answered by the fact that the vessel tacked at Cuckhold's Head—what would she be doing there if she was not bound for St. John's, and how much nearer must she have come to look for a pilot? After careful consideration of the evidence, I can only find one satisfactory reason for Vinicombe's not having put a pilot aboard the Spanish vessel that evening, and that is the reason given by the pilot Kavanagh — he (Vinicombe) wanted all his crew to tow in the English schooner, and the money they got for hobbling went direct into their own pockets and not in the Pilot's fund. In no other way can I account for Vinicombe's wilful negligence in not putting a pilot aboard the Spanish brigantine on that evening.

As regards the charge against pilot boat No. 4, William Gallishew, the case is very plain and simple. It was his duty to have been outside with his boat at sunset, or when Fort Amherst light was lit; but instead of being on duty at the appointed time, he did not leave Mr. Shea's wharf until at least 9 that evening, and when he got to the narrows, instead of looking about for vessels, he coolly tied on to a net-buoy two gun-shots from the mouth of the Harbor, and remained there all night. If he had been on duty at the appointed time, he must have seen the Spanish vessel, as she tacked at Cuckhold's Head just after the light was lit, as shown by Moore's and Dearin's evidence.

If Pilots are allowed to conduct themselves in this manner, they are only a trap and a snare to the unfortunate foreign vessels approaching our port. The case of the *Mayguezana* appears to me a most monstrous case of neglect. Here a foreign vessel comes to within a half a mile of the entrance to the harbor with her flags flying asking for a pilot, speaks to two fishermen's boats to see if they will pilot her in, and finally, after exerting every effort to get admission to the port under the guidance of a pilot, has at last to give it up and put to sea again, exposed to delay and possibly to danger, simply because one pilot wants to make a few dollars extra for his men, and another pilot is either too lazy or unfit to go to sea. I have not gone particularly into the question as to whether there was contributory negligence on the part of the Spanish Captain - want of seamanship on his part, even if proved in the clearest manner, would not in the least degree exonerate the pilots.

You will note in the evidence that Vinicombe blames Gallishew and Gallishew blames Vinicombe. Vinicombe, however, who *saw* the vessel in daylight had a spare pilot and the means of putting him aboard, and who appears not to have cared or troubled himself in any way about the Spaniard, and did not even tell Gallishew's boat about her, is in my opinion the most to blame. Vinicombes's case is a wilful neglect of duty; Gallishew's a case of utter carelessness and negligence - he never *saw* any vessel and he never *tried* to see any one, and from sunset until at least 9 if not 10 he was away from his post altogether."

The Commission of Pilots rendered this decision after reading Judge Prowse's report;

> "....the Commissioners have awarded the following punishment, vix: To William Vinicombe, three months suspension.......there are some extenuating circumstances in his case, inasmuch as he had with his crew undertaken to assist the *Queen of Clippers*, and that the boat had arrived when the night boat should have been available to put a pilot on board the *Mayaguezana*. Vinicombe bears a good character for general conduct and sobriety. To William Gallishew.....six months suspension, he being,......the most culpable in having failed to be at his post at the proper hour, and not until the night had too far advance to enable him to render any assistance to vessels in the offing. Had he communicated with Vinicombe's boat, which he could easily have done...he might have ascertained the presence of a white painted vessel outside.....and if boarded by Gallishew......the melancholy disaster.....would in all human probability have been averted."[42]

On August 28th, the body of Captain Fioll's nine year old daughter was found.

One month after the enquiry into the *Mayaguezana* disaster, the following four sections were added to the existing bye-laws for the guidance of pilots;

> "No. 1 - That the division of Pilotage Monies between any two or more Boats be prohibited, and any infringement of this Bye-Law shall forfeit the Licences of the Pilots belonging to the Boats making or receiving any such division of Pilotage Monies.
>
> No. 2 - In the case of the suspension of any Pilot, a like Penalty shall be imposed on any Pilot or Pilots, belonging to the same Boat, who shall allow to the suspended Pilot any portion of the earnings of the Boat during such suspension.
>
> No. 3 - That it shall be compulsory for each Boat in rotation, to take Night Service from kindling of the Light on Fort Amherst every evening till extinguishing of the same on the following morning, at which time the Boat on duty for the night shall be relieved by another of the Pilot Boats going on duty for the day, such relief service shall also be undertaken by each of the Boats in regular rotation.
>
> No. 4 - It shall be the duty of the Master of each Pilot Boat to render to the Chairman of the Commissioners of Pilots, every three months, a true and correct account of all Monies received by him, as the earnings of the Boat, under his charge for Pilotage of Vessels together with a correct list of the Vessels so Piloted." [43]

Four More Tragic Drownings

In February, 1878, two drownings resulting from a storm occurred in the two little communities of Blackhead and Freshwater Bay near St. John's. Both deaths were very similar in that each boy was engaged in trying to salvage wreckage and gear swept away by the tides and strong gale that day. Both boys, one a son of William Haley in Blackhead and the other a son of William Walsh in Freshwater Bay, were down by the water with their younger brothers when a sea carried them away. Young Haley (probably Healey, as that is a Blackhead name), walked out when a wave receded and was warned by his brother that a wave was coming. Instead of jumping for the shore, he sprang upon a rock nearby and the incoming sea engulfed him up to his waist. The shock of the cold water must have tumbled him as he lost his balance and he was swept away and badly bounced around against the rock by the rough seas. When Haley's body was recovered there were severe contusions on it. Walsh's body was not recovered.[44]

Another drowning took place that year, this time in the Narrows. Captain John Masters of the English schooner *Pass-By* and Captain Date of the *Mary Ann* decided to go outside the harbour on Tuesday, September 17th, to catch a few fish just for relaxation and sport. When they got out into the Narrows, a sudden squall struck the boat and capsized it. Capt. Date swam a short distance and was picked up by the pilot John Vinicombe who happened to be nearby in his boat. Although, Capt. Masters was a strong man only 33 years old, he was a poor swimmer. Vinicombe managed to get him out of the water but Masters was so exhausted that he died almost immediately. He left a wife and three children in England. He had a Masonic funeral the following day and was buried in the Episcopal Cemetery in St. John's.[45]

The year 1879 started out sadly enough with a another casualty in the Narrows. On Thursday afternoon, January 2nd, the brigantine *Mayflower*, belonging to Mr. March was being towed out by a tug. As a crewman named McGimley was cat-heading (hauling up) the anchor, he fell overboard and never rose again. It was thought that he was struck by the vessel. When his body was found the next day, the marks on it showed that he had received severe injury in his fall from the bollards of his ship. McGimley was a native of St. John's and left a wife and several children.[46]

Not Always Doom and Gloom

Back in the days before television and all the associated electronic entertainment, the people of St. John's found other interests. One source of diversion was the activity in and outside the harbour. There was always something happening to draw everyone's attention to the water front. On July 8, 1879, it was two young men named Barnes and Hughes who had challenged each other to a boat race. They started from the Goodfellow & Co. wharf in the harbour and rowed to the Chain Rock and back. Hughes made it in 20 minutes and won while being cheered on by nearly 200 spectators.[47]

Meanwhile, just outside the harbour, Freshwater Bay was alive with squid and a dozen bankers were waiting to get the bait fish. People up on Signal Hill had a great view of the bay and the many schooners loading and heading back to the Grand Banks.

On Wednesday, August 6th, a fisherman captured a 5 foot shark in the Narrows. He brought it to the wharf of J & W Boyd.[48] No doubt many hundreds of curious townsfolk traveled to the wharf to see the unusual catch.

St. John's has been the starting point for many adventurers attempting to cross the Atlantic in all sizes and shapes of crafts. People were hurrying to the waterfront to see such a craft entering the Narrows one evening in August, 1879. The whole town assembled to greet the *Uncle Sam*, owned and navigated by J. Goldsmid and his wife. The 18 foot vessel was going to cross the Atlantic to England. The Goldsmids left on August 12th and on September 19th were rescued at sea and the *Uncle Sam* was scuttled in their failed attempt to cross the Atlantic.[49]

All the citizens of St. John's were hurrying to the waterfront on November 10th to see the steamship *Arizona*. The 5,600 ton ship was one of the fastest and the largest (next to the *Great Eastern*), steamships on the Atlantic. It was unusual for so large a ship to come into the port unexpectedly at 8 a.m. and hundreds of people gathered at the wharf of the Hon. Ambrose Shea to see her and find out why she had come in. The front of the ship showed that the *Arizona* had been in a terrible accident. While en route across the Atlantic Ocean, the ship had crashed into an iceberg in the fog about 300 miles from St. John's. About twenty feet of the bow had been destroyed but beyond the first compartment she held no water and luckily didn't sink. She immediately headed for St. John's, passengers and crew alike very thankful for their escape from a watery grave. The Guion Line steamer left December 1st, after repairs were made to her.[50]

The Narrows blocked with ice and iceberg (City of St. John's Archives)

Going Swiling off the Narrows

During the winter of 1879-1880, the ice was once again blocking the Narrows. On Wednesday, February 18, 1880 the S.S.*Nimrod* spent all day trying to get in through the thick ice with no success. On Thursday, she was still stuck when the tug *Hercules* went out and managed to butt through the ice to clear water. The *Hercules* then returned in the same channel and backed up to the schooner *Julia Grace*, took her in tow beyond Cape Spear. Returning, the tug took the barquentine *Harriet* anchored at the edge of the ice, and brought her into Bowrings wharf. The *Nimrod* was then able to get in through the path cut by the busy tug.[51]

Although a nuisance to shipping, the ice was the source of much excitement, entertainment and source of employment in the Spring of 1880. Alas, it was to prove the source of much sorrow also. During that Spring, the people of St. John's and environs spent many days up on Signal Hill and along the shoreline watching all the activity out on the ice. Besides ships stuck in ice, there were hundreds of seals and the local people took advantage of earning a few dollars from the killing of these northern visitors.

The Royal Gazette reported on Tuesday, March 30, 1880 that quite an excitement was created the day before by the news that a number of seals were seen outside the heads. As soon as word got about, men armed with gaffs and bats went out and before nightfall had landed about 200 young harps on the South Side.

The excitement had drawn many visitors to the vicinity of the Narrows to watch the hunt. Two boys named Keough and Power with a few of their friends went out to the North Battery to see the men catching seals. While the boys were going along the cliff, Power and Keough slipped and fell about 50 feet into the water below. Power, who was older and stronger, managed to to get to shore without much injury. But Keough, age 8 or 9 got badly beaten by the rocks and may have been dead before he even struck the water. The body was recovered and taken to his father' home, Michael Keough who was a shoemaker on Water Street.[52]

The next day, Tuesday, Jonathon Taylor, one of the sealers, discovered a dead body on the ice four miles off the Narrows. There was a gun besides the man and it was later confirmed that he was Martin Hogan, one of several missing men from Northern Bay who had been lost on the ice while out sealing a week earlier. Judge Prowse was informed of the discovery and ordered a constable and a party of men to go out and retrieve the body. At 2:00 p.m. Sgt. Lacey and a "posse" of men left from Fort Townsend and tramped 4 miles over the ice to the body. They had a very difficult time getting to the corpse and before they got back, some of the men had fallen into the water getting thoroughly wet. Another body was found on Wednesday by two men out sealing near Small Point, Quidi Vidi. Thomas Boyle and William Brien of St. John's discovered the body of Luke Nevill who died of exposure after being stuck out on the ice all night.

The Evening Telegram, observed the following on Saturday;

> "At noon yesterday we observed a young Nimrod making for the ice. He wore a brown duck overall and a broad belt around his waist from which gleamed a terrible-looking knife. A lot of harness was rolled round his body, at his heels trotted two huge Newfoundland dogs, and in his hands he carried a gaff and several other *necessary* articles. We have not yet heard how many fierce old harps he captured." [53]

Men and boys kept going out on the ice and the accidents kept happening. On Sunday, April 4, 1880, there were dozens of people outside the Narrows when the wind changed causing the ice to loosen and drift; a dangerous situation for all those on the ice. James McGinn and Michael Sinnott were out when the ice started moving off from the shore. They both jumped into the icy water and swam to Small Point, a distance of 15-20 yards. To the North of the Narrows, two boys stepped off the ice and got on shore at a spot called Green Gulch (near Sugar Loaf), which was an almost perpendicular cliff. They climbed up but got stuck just before they reached the top. By now they were both exhausted and to add to their predicament, they couldn't go back down on the ice for it had moved off. While in this hazardous position, they were observed by several men nearby who hurried to their rescue. The men took off their suspenders, tied them together, then reached over the brow of the cliff and lowered the "rope" to the boys who came up one at a time assisted by the suspender rope.

Still on the same day, a more serious accident befell a group of men and boys from various parts of the city who had gone out over the ice to kill a few seals earlier in the day. Only the surnames of the sealing group were given; they were two Fowler brothers from Cook's Town, a man Power from Carter's Hill, Chislett and his son, Puddister, O'Toole and his son from Hoyles Town, Doyle, Walsh, Murray, Nugent and Anderson. All were trapped on the ice when it started to break up and drift away. *The Evening Telegram* reported the next day that only Puddister, O'Toole and his son succeeded in getting ashore and that little hope was entertained for the recovery of the rest. The paper also stated that Martin Murray had fallen into the water and disappeared before his companions could save him. However, more information was given the following day in *The Royal Gazette.* Apparently, the government ordered the steamer *Hercules* out to search for the missing men but it returned unsuccessful. Once again the vessel was dispatched but before she returned the sealing steamer *Walrus* entered the Narrows with one of the missing men, Murray, on board. Martin Murray who had been reported drowned, accounted for six other men who were safe on board the *Esquimaux.* The *Hercules* finally returned with the rest of the men including those who were rescued by the *Esquimaux.* The men and boys had a hard time out on the ice and the younger O'Toole was nearly exhausted when rescued.[54]

Later that month the S. S. *Caspian* had an accident which didn't involve ice but fog. The *Caspian*, a mail steamer of the Allan Line was making her first direct run of the season from Liverpool, England. While steering for the Narrows in a dense fog and without a pilot, the ship ran on the rocks off the Northern Head known as the Wash Balls. Her bows were broken below the water line and she started to leak badly.She managed to get off the rocks immediately and steamed into the harbour and to the wharf of the ship's agent, Hon. A. Shea. The ship had settled in the water considerably by then and when the hatches were removed, a large quantity of water was seen in the hold. A lot of the cargo was damaged and the passengers, mail and some other cargo had to continue on to Halifax by the *Newfoundland* which had arrived in port the same day.[55]

Talk of a Steam Yacht for the Pilots

By 1880, the port of St. John's had several tugs such as the *Dauntless, Favourite* and *Daisy*. The latter choose an unusual way to get a tow one day in May. The *Daisy* was just outside the Narrows on May 18th when she collided with a schooner. The tug caused so much injury that she had to take the schooner in tow and brought her into the harbour where she was grounded full of water.[56]

All the accidents and near misses to shipping in and out of port (see appendix) and disabled vessels arriving almost daily, must have prompted one of the pilots to write this letter to the editor in June;

"Our Pilotage Facilities.

Sir, - In a maritime port like St. John's it is a matter of importance that the pilotage facilities should be commensurate with the wants of the trade. Besides owning a fine fleet of foreign-going vessels ourselves, which are engaged in transporting our produce all over the world, we employ to a large extent, transitory shipping, bringing to us salt, provisions, building material, &c., from many different markets abroad. To our own merchants it is often a great consideration to have an expected vessel make port quickly, in order that she may get quick dispatch again for some leading fish market. Oftentimes a few hours in getting into St. John's, or even a single hour, cause all the difference between "making a good market", or the reverse. In the case of foreign ships, our immediate coast is so liable to be obscured by fogs - suddenly tilting down upon the land and confusing the seaman's eye as to the coast-line - that, under such circumstances, vessels often pass the mouth of the Harbor without making it; while repeated instances of accidents to vessels and the loss of human lives have occurred in consequence of our want of pilotage facilities.

We have at present fifteen able-bodied pilots on the active list, who have at their disposal four whale boats wherewith to dare the stormy seas in the execution of their calling. In these, when the sea is at all tempestuous, a condition of frequent experience about the Narrows; it is impossible for them to venture far out without risking their lives. They have therefore to depend upon boarding the incoming vessel after the latter have approached sufficiently near the land to relieve them from at least some of the perils that pilotage is intended to protect them from. When the fog comes down, or thick weather sets in, the inward-bound ship and the pilot boat are equally baffled; and at such a crisis, when pilotage is really of most value, it is not, on our coast available at all!

It is not to be assumed from the foregoing remarks that any blame is attachable to anyone on account of this state of affairs. But at the same time, the present is a state of affairs that is not creditable to us as a maritime people, who are ourselves so largely interested in the safety and quick passage of our vessels.

As a remedy for the want, it is suggested that a small steam yacht should be purchased and placed at the disposal of our hardy pilots, in which they could go a good distance off to sea, and from which they could put a pilot on board any incoming vessels before the necessity of a return to port. The cost of such an appliance would be absolutely small, and the saving it would effect (in many ways) in a single year would pay for itself over and over again. It is certain that our local ship-owners would subscribe for its purchase, our insurance companies and pilots would help, and the cost, thus made up, would bear lightly on all.

Yours truly, No. 4 Pilot Boat."[57]

Sudden Death while Rowing Through the Narrows

A Magisterial Enquiry before Judge Prowse on February 7, 1882, related this sudden death in the Narrows;

"........Charles Stone, of St. John's, fisherman, upon his oath stated: " I have known the deceased John Chalk for the past twenty-five years, and he lived in George's Town. Yesterday evening, about 3 o'clock, the deceased and I went out in a boat to Cuckhold's Cove for the purpose of shooting sea-birds. We shot several birds. About six o'clock, when we were returning home, we got as far as Chain Rock, where we waited for some time to allow the slob (loose ice) which was passing out to clear away. As soon as a favorable time offered we started rowing again as hard as we could, as the wind was blowing strongly, when the deceased fell suddenly from the seat upon which he was sitting and exclaimed "Oh Charley!" I then took in my oar and lifted him up, believing he had only fainted; but I soon found that he was quite dead. When I took him in my arms I spoke to him, telling him to rouse himself; but he made no reply nor ever spoke after he fell. I then laid him down in the bottom of the boat, during which time I drifted some distance out the Narrows, and having no person to assist me, I had much difficulty in reaching the south side of the Narrows, near the Light House. Here I was assisted by Thomas Moore and afterwards by the Pilots, Thomas Nurse and crew who brought me ashore. The body was than conveyed to the morgue by the police. I know the deceased was ailing for some time past, but do not know that he was attended by a doctor. He was a very stout man, fifty-five years of age, and leaves a widow and one child."[58]

People walking on the ice out through the Narrows (MHA)

Ice-Bound

It was probably the extra exertion trying to get through the slob ice which was in the Narrows which caused the death of John Chalk. Two weeks later, the ice was still causing trouble for shipping. Ships were trying to get out through the Narrows while more were stuck at the entrance trying to get in.. The Dundee sealing steamers, *Arctic*, *Aurora, Resolute* and the Western mail boat, *Plover* had arrived and hundreds of men were engaged cutting a channel to get the vessels in. There were 126 icebergs visible from Cape Spear, one being 2 miles long.

In St. John's harbour, the sealing fleet was really to get underway and numerous reports were told of men and boys falling into the harbour through the ice. Around the same time, the brigantine *Fedore* was forced onto the rocks at Cape Spear. During all this activity someone from *The Evening Telegram* strolled up Signal Hill at 6:30 a.m. on Saturday March 18, 1812 and wrote about what he saw;

"......The weather was fine and clear with keen frost and a light northeast breeze......the "signal of disease" fluttering from the Small Pox Hospital and a timid rabbit bounding over the snow near the ice-covered edge of St. George's Pond. On reaching the Block House the view that broke upon us was...."awfully sublime". Below lay the city just awakening.....smoke darted heaven ward from a thousand chimneys......Seaward an illimitable stretch of ice met the eyes, with nothing to break the monotony beyond a massive berg here and there glittering in the sunlight, and a few "imprisoned" ships. Just above the horizon, about forty miles N.E., we could see, with the aid of a glass....the *Merlin*. The vessel seemed to be working to the eastward, and from her movements.....probable she was picking up seals. Some three miles S.S.E. of the Narrows lay the s.s. *Resolute*. She had steam up and all her fore-and-aft sails set, but the ice appeared to be too heavy to admit of her making any progress whatever. On the rocks near Cape Spear could be seen the stranded brigantine "Fedore", and about a quarter of a mile inside of Black Head we observed the "Amanda", firmly locked in the ice, but in no immediate danger. That's all!"

Tragedy Near Flower Rock Shoals

A couple of weeks later in April 1812, at a spot known as Flower Rock Shoals, near the Fort Amherst Lighthouse, the writer of the last article would have witnessed a tragic accident and a heroic rescue in which a little girl was involved. The blaring headline "Fatal Accident Near Fort Amherst" preceded this sad story;

> "A melancholy accident, involving the death of a poor fellow named John Fitzgerald, occurred last evening only a short distance from Fort Amherst. Between five and six o'clock a boat with a crew of four men, named James Byrne, William Fitzgerald, Thomas Murphy and John Fitzgerald, left here for Black Head. The weather being fine and the sea smooth, no apprehension of danger was entertained by any of them until they had rounded the South Head near Fort Amherst, when from some cause, not yet explained to us, the boat suddenly capsized and all hands were thrown into the water. Fortunately, a little girl named Minnie Moore, whose parents live near the Light House, happened to witness the accident, and, with remarkable sagacity for a child only 6 years of age, ran in breathless haste to her father and informed him of what had occurred. Mr. Moore immediately rushed out of the house, and, looking in the direction indicated by the child, was horrified at the spectacle before him. There he beheld four men struggling for their lives, and to increase his anxiety, he could see no means of rendering them such prompt assistance as their extremely dangerous position demanded. However, without a moment's hesitation, he did the best he could under the circumstances. Hastily alarming the inmates of the Light House, Mr. Moore ran bareheaded to the residence of the Messrs. King, about a quarter of a mile distant, and told them to get in their boat, "for God's sake", and pull to the rescue, at the same time informing them that there were "four men drowning back of the Head." Meanwhile, Mrs. Moore went down to the land-wash, and, getting as close as she could to the men in the water, heedless of the waves that dashed over her, she first assured them of approaching help and then did all in her power to encourage them in their struggle for life. As she stood there, one of the men, John Fitzgerald, despite her cheering words, became exhausted, and, bidding her good-bye, threw up his arms and disappeared beneath the waves. The sight was a sad one, indeed, and Mrs. Moore has been deeply affected by it ever since. Immediately after this tragic incident, two boats dashed round the Head - one belonging to the Messrs. King and the other from Black Head. James Byrne and William Fitzgerald were rescued by the former, and Mr. Moore and the Messrs. King saved Thomas Murphy, together with the boat and provisions. It is admitted by all that had it not been for the great presence of mind exemplified by Minnie Moore, and her father's promptitude in rendering assistance, not one of the four men would have escaped. The deceased was a sober industrious young man about 27 years of age."[59]

Minnie Margaret Moore was the adopted and only child of Bridget and Thomas Moore. Her father was assistant keeper at Fort Amherst from 1869-1906. Less than a year later, little Minnie died at the lighthouse on February 25, 1883; she was only 7 ½ years old.

In late summer, 1882, another tragic drowning occurred just outside the Narrows. On Tuesday afternoon, August 15th, four young boys were seen happily going out the Narrows in their little boat. Three of the boys were sons of Captain Robinson R.N. and the other a son of Rev. Arthur Wood. There was hardly a breath of air in the harbour as they ventured outside the Narrows in Capt. Robinson's boat. However, when they got outside the heads, a sudden squall upset the craft, throwing all four boys into the water. They all clung to the boat except 13 year old Thomas Robinson. His 16 year old brother George, who was an expert swimmer, took Thomas on his back and started to swim for the shore. After about 20 minutes, young Thomas was chilled and exhausted and slipped off his brother's back and disappeared below the water. George made it back to the boat to which the two other boys were still clinging. The struggle for life had been witnessed by fishermen nearby who hurried to the rescue. The dead boy and his brother had only arrived in St. John's a few weeks earlier from school in England to spend their summer vacation with their parents. They were going to return to England the next day.[60]

Schooners tack out the Narrows past the Fort Amherst Lighthouse (CNS Archives)

A Schooner Capsizes off Fort Amherst

Around 7:30 a.m., on Thursday, May 31, 1883 the tug-boat *Cabot* was seen slowly steaming around the Southern Head towing a vessel with her masts flat on the water and the sails going up and down with the waves. This spectacle was observed by many curious onlookers as the tug struggled in through the Narrows and up the harbour with its unusual tow. It was later learned that the schooner in tow or drag, was the *M. Monroe*, which had been recently built at Exploits by a Mr. Dalton for the man whose name the craft bore. The *M. Monroe* had sailed from Exploits a week before and after pushing against head winds most of the way, had arrived outside the Narrows at 6 a.m. She was about to enter port when a sudden violent squall swept off the land about 300 yards from the Fort Amherst lighthouse and knocked the craft clean over on her beam ends. The captain and crew saw her going over and scrambled up on the side of her in time to escape a wetting or worse. They were there only five minutes when Captain Green in his tug came hurrying to the rescue. He passed a line on board the schooner, took the men off and proceeded to tow her into port. After she was taken inside, the little vessel was righted and no damage was noticed. Their only loss was a bit of deck cargo which had drifted away. Considering that the vessel and her cargo were not insured, they may have gotten away cheap with just the bill for towage.[61]

Cahill Point Heroes: A Near Tragedy in Hay Cove

An incoming schooner nearly met its doom in the Narrows in August 1883 and some fishermen living near Cahill's Point, now the western end of the Fort Amherst Boat Basin, were the heroes of the day;

> "A small craft owned by a man named Avery arrived to Messrs. P& L Tessier's last evening, right in the midst of the gale, and after a very narrow escape at the entrance of the harbor. She left Grates Cove early on Wednesday morning with about 250 quintals of fish, bound "straight for this port;" but when fairly out in the mouth of Conception Bay the wind dropped off, and her progress was necessarily very slow until near Torbay, when the severe Southeast gale of yesterday broke upon Skipper Avery and his crew, threatening to send them all to "the bottom of the deep blue sea." ......On several occasions the sea swept over everything.....the wind rapidly veered until it blew from the Eastward, when they were enabled to get round Sugar Loaf and, soon after, to reach the less turbulent waters of the Narrows. But here the greatest danger of all awaited them. The wind was very erratic, or "baffling," and the difficulty of beating in without running into the breakers was next thing to insuperable. Still the craft continued to work remarkably well under the circumstances until Hay Cove was reached, when she misstayed and her situation became extremely critical. One of the anchors was immediately let go; but this last resource proved unequal to the emergency, and in a moment or two more she was thumping against the rocks. Here, she would have been reduced to a total wreck, no doubt, but for the gallant conduct of John King, Patrick Murphy, James Hogan and William Hunt, fishermen on Mr. King's Room, South Side. These noble-hearted men were in the mess-room, taking their tea, when they became aware of the danger to which their fellow "toilers of the sea" were exposed.......they arose from the table, seized their hats and ran to a boat at the landing hard by, into which they immediately jumped and put out for the schooner. On getting alongside they found all hands at their wits' end. One of the crew had taken advantage of the

A ship on the rocks in Hay Cove below Signal Hill (Joey Power)

craft's proximity to the rocks when tacking on the other side of the Narrows and jumped ashore. The others were so completely exhausted that they could do little.......The four men....... offered their assistance.....went to work with a will, and finally succeeded, not only in getting the vessel off, but in beating her in the harbor and mooring her at the wharf of Messrs. P.& L. Tessier. While pulling to the rescue, they were in imminent danger of losing their own lives; and on two or three occasions their boat was nearly capsized by the force of the wind and sea.........We are proud of the country that can produce such men, and contend that their names ought to be registered among the heroes of the nineteenth century."[62]

Running the Gauntlet of Ice, Fog and Darkness

It would have been an intimidating task to enter the dark Narrows before there were any lighted harbour buoys; the Chain Rock light would not be established until 1925. There would not have been as many lights in the city or along the Narrows to outline the way and the Fort Amherst light was not as bright as today. Also, there was no radar or electronic devises to aid the passing vessels. The Narrows was a difficult channel to negotiate in daytime and worse in the dark. The following events for the year 1884, are typical of the activity and danger vessels faced before navigational aids made the Narrows safer.

On Monday, January 28th , 1884 two vessels approached the mouth of the Narrows around 4 p.m.; the barquentine *Maranee* coming from Trapani (Sicily) to Goodridge & Sons and the *Flora* from, New York to Munn & Co. The *Maranee* kept tacking across the mouth of the harbour trying to attract a tug but had no success. She was coated with ice and had to stay outside all night in that condition and only managed to get a foothold in the Narrows at 9 a.m. the following morning. She dropped anchor and awaited a tow. Luckily for both vessels, no high gale of wind prevailed or there may have been another tragedy to report. Where were the tugs and pilots?

A similar incident had happened back in September when the S.S. *Nova Scotian* had appeared off the Narrows at 12:40 a.m. and started throwing up rockets to attract attention. She got safely in after an hour but the the editor of that account stated that the captains of the Allan boats dreaded to enter the Narrows or even approach our shores on dark nights.

Thick fog didn't help shipping either, the S.S. *Waldensian* was outside the harbour for 6 days in April waiting to get in. The fog lifted for a few hours and she made her dash through the Narrows bringing a 1000 tons of goods from Glasgow and Liverpool. While she was outside she must have been aware of the icebergs around the coast. Captain Edward White of the S.S. *Hector* arrived from a second trip from the seal fishery and reported an iceberg 3 miles long and 60 feet high with a perfectly level top, off shore in the shipping lane. He warned his fellow seafarers to beware as the iceberg could be easily mistaken for land in foggy weather. It was dangerously near the local whale and seal fishing fleets.

In June a huge iceberg was off Bay Bulls and the schooner *Eugenie* struck it and had to be towed to St. John's in a disabled condition The same iceberg decided to pay the Narrows a visit a few days later, nearly blocking the entrance. It proved a menace to the *Weaver Belle* on Friday, June 6th as the schooner was arriving from Cadiz with a cargo of salt for John Steer. Around 3:30 that afternoon, the vessel was trying to make the harbour in a thick fog, unaware of the presence of the iceberg. Suddenly she ran right against the huge ice island, carrying away her jibboom, bowsprit and doing other damage and giving the crew and captain an awful fright. As soon as she got clear, the pumps were tried and it was found that the vessel was not leaky. She succeeded in getting into port shortly after the accident.[63]

A Sad Parade through the Narrows

On July 26th, 1884 a parade of vessels slowly and sadly steamed out through the Narrows as the Greely Relief Expedition took their departure for Portsmouth, New Hampshire at 10 a.m. Following the *Thetis, Alert* and *Bear* were the local steam launches with some of St. John's prominent citizens on board. The tugs accompanied the ships nearly as far as Cape Spear where they dipped their flags in respect and returned to port. A few days before, the return of the Greely Expedition had created "an unwonted stir" in St. John's as the four steamers came in with 19 dead on board; the *Loch Garry* had come in with the other ships then. Only six men survived the ill-fated northern expedition, Lt. Adolphus Greely and five others while 19 had died. The three departing ships took 12 of the bodies with them.[64]

Fatal Accident off Cuckhold's Head

The fickle winds outside the Narrows were blamed for the drowning of a young girl on August 25, 1884.

> "Another accident last evening between 5 and 6 o'clock, on the water, involving the loss of one life, swells the list of drowning casualties which have been unhappily more common this season than we have ever known them to be in previous seasons. In the present instance a seaman of the *Racer*, named Leggatt, was out in a sail-boat with two girls, named Mary Jane Hollett and Catherine Sheaves, and was half a mile off Cuckhold's Head, when a sudden squall struck the little craft and upset her, precipitating all three into the water. The accident was observed from Fort Amherst Light-house, the keeper of which signalled the tug-boat *Favorite*, Captain Parsons, which was then passing out the Narrows, and communicated a knowledge of the disaster, indicating also its whereabouts. Parsons put his boat under full speed for the spot and succeeded in rescuing Leggatt and the girl Catherine Sheaves. Leggatt, with considerable heroism, managed to keep both girls afloat for a length of time, but his strength failing, he had to abandon the poor girl Howlett, who was drowned. Want of due care and proper management had its share in contributing to this disaster, and with such a party Legatt should not have proceeded alone without an assistant to help him in attending to the sails. It is also well that strangers and our own people too, should understand that this harbor and offing is a most unsafe one for boating with sails. The wind doesn't blow with that steadiness characteristic of places where the land around is level, but comes down from the high hills in fitful gusts, so that a boat which at one moment may be sailing at a safe angle to the water, and the next instant have her rail plunged under the surface. Sail-boats should be well ballasted and those in charge be always on the alert to let go the sheets."[65]

The tug later towed in the boat which had capsized. Before the accident, Leggatt had taken down the sail and tried to row back in but making no progress, he again hoisted sail; the tragic accident happened after that. Mary Jane was the second daughter of William and Rebecca Hollett; she was only 22 years old.

A sailboat in trouble near Cuckhold's Head (Joey Power)

Trying to get a "Hobble"

The local tugs were always in competition with each other trying to get a tow job to earn some money. Sometimes they would hang around outside the Narrows or the Heads as it was sometimes called, scanning St. John's Bay for possible business. The writer of this item in *The Evening Telegram* on May 13, 1885 painted a humorous picture of an encounter between a persistent tug and a reluctant steamer;

> "While the steamer *Leopard* was tacking, on Monday night, to a position well windward of the harbor, so as to avoid being caught on the lee shore inside of Cape Spear, a tug-boat hailed her, the captain of which modestly offered to tow the crippled sealer into port for £150. "I don't suppose you could see any green in my eye at that distance," replied Captain Dawe. "Well, we'll make it £125, seeing as how things turned out indifferently this spring." "The great trouble in dealing with a tug-boat man like you is that you're too cheap." "One more and my last offer, captain: you better take my line and we'll call the job square at a round hundred." "I'll try a few more tacks," said Dawe. Meantime the tug-boat kept following the steamer in and out, and at every tack the ship gained a nearer footing in the Narrows, and at every "tack" the tug-boat man abated his demands by ten pounds. At last more sail was put on the *Leopard*, and the tug-boat man, seeing that his prey was on the hand of escaping, offered to bring her in for thirty pounds. "Not much: I'm too near an anchorage to pay extra money now; call it ordinary rates and it's a bargain!" "Well ordinary rates let it be; pass us your line!" and in handsome style the tug-boat towed the *Leopard* in."

There were no shipwrecks to report in the summer of 1885. The squid came right in the harbour in July and even washed ashore on the sand in Gill's Cove where some men picked up a tubfull of them. Out at Cape Spear on July 29, 1885 an unusual incident happened. John and William Haley (Healey) of Black Head were fishing on Old Harry Rock (a submerged rock just off the bill off the cape), when a sword fish attacked their boat. It drove two holes through the bottom taking three bits of timber from the keel. The startled men shoved their clothes into the holes to keep from sinking. Then a thrasher, a fish which usually accompanies swordfish, rose out of the water and flicked its tail near the boat. The thrasher's tail hit the end of the mast which was lying along the boat partly projecting over the stern, and sent it spinning in the air! Mr. James Healey's skiff had to come to their assistance.[66]

The Summer of 1886

All of the following items were gleamed from *The Evening Telegram* covering the months of July, August and September, 1886. Every year the local papers reported similar events, too many to be included in this book. The following is just a sample of the activity which took place in and around the Narrows every year.

On July 8th, a fishing skiff, laden with caplin, belonging to Mr. Shea of Pouch Cove, capsized while beating in the Narrows. The occupants, a man and a boy were thrown into the water but managed to cling onto the boat until a tug-boat came to their rescue.

Squid made their appearance in the harbour on July 19th and hundreds of them were jigged from Job's Wharf. The men and boys then sold the squid to bankers at 10¢ a dozen.

On July 20th, a black whale was captured by a whaling crew off port under the command of Frederick Lewis and towed in by the tug *Favorite* to Brooking's wharf. The whale carcass was towed out to sea a week later by Charles Lewis because it was a "source of mortal offense to the dwellers above Clapp's Cove and also to the salt-water bathers."

On Saturday afternoon, August 21st, the barquentine *Spark* was going to sea. The captain of a English schooner *Isabella Helen* decided to accompany Captain Skaardon as far as the Narrows. The captain had a sail-boat tied onto the *Spark* to return to port. After he left the ship and had cast off, he noticed that the mast of his boat was entangled in a rope which dragged over the ship's stern. In an instant the boat capsized and sank, hurling the captain who couldn't swim, into the water. Fortunately, the disaster was seen from the *Spark;* William Cantwell and John Gallishaw, Jr. jumped into their pilot boat and rescued the drowning man.

In September, another rash of accidents were reported by *The Evening Telegram.* On September 3, 1886, Mr. Harvey's sail-yacht was well out in the Narrows when the wind suddenly veered to the northeast. An eddy of wind broke the mast off but the boat didn't overturn due to its broad build. There were several people on board at the time and they were towed in by a tug. On the ninth, two schooners, outward bound were in collision off the Narrows.

If anyone was looking out towards the Narrows on Monday, September 27th, they would have seen the *Lady Agnes* crippling into port. Captain Piper had left Trinity a few days earlier and all was going well until they were 40 miles off Baccalieu where they hit an iceberg. They had to fight headwinds all the way to St. John's in their damaged craft.

Two Pilots are Taken for a Ride!

Two local pilots had a lot to talk about in October, 1886, after they finally got home;

> "A "strange, eventful experience" was that which befell two pilots named Gallishaw this morning. At the present moment they on board an American schooner, the *John Ingram*, bound to Boston. The misadventure is something out of the usual run of accidents that happen to these staunch and seamanlike guides to vessels seeking this port.......the two men in question were on board the schooner named piloting her through the Narrows, and were in tow of the tug *Favorite*; their boat, in which was a youth named Lewis, was held to the schooner by a painter, and was following in the schooner's wake. Coming to sea immediately after them was the banking schooner *Lavinia*, which swayed to and fro in the tremendous sea thrown up by the Northeaster. Both crafts were passing through the Narrows at the time. Fearing that the *Lavinia*, which was running free and approaching dangerously close, with her main-sail jibbing wildly, might bear down and crush their boat, the pilots lengthened the painter. In doing so, the rope slipped from the grasp of the man who was doing the work, and the boat, with the boy in it, drifted off into the "yeast of waters." To rescue the lad, Capt. Parsons had to slip his hawser at a point short of the usual distance, but as the schooner had seaway before her, there was no danger in doing this. He picked up the lad, who was white with fright, and the boat, and then steamed after the schooner to take off the pilots. He brought the tug's prow close up to the latter's side, a task of some difficulty in so heavy a sea, and wrenched some of the iron sheathing on the boat's bow while doing so, but he gave the two pilots a chance to leap aboard. The latter "refused the leap," however, and this is how it happened that they are now on board the *John Ingram*, bound to Boston."[67]

High above the waters of the Narrows on Signal Hill, this terrible accident occurred two days later on Tuesday, October 26th;

"Richard Moore, who was killed yesterday by falling into Ross's Valley, the cavernous depth that yawns beneath one's feet on the sea-side of the ridge on which is built the Block-house, Signal Hill, was an old well known resident of Hoylestown, and was about 69 years of age. The tragic occurrence was caused by an attack of epilepsy, to which deceased was subject. He was hauling a load of material from an old building, which is being dismantled, when, it is supposed, he was suddenly seized with a fit, and the violent spasmodic motions that followed, edged the unfortunate man nearer and nearer the brink of the precipice, till at length he fell in and rolled from shelf to shelf to a fearful distance down. No human eye marked the catastrophe; none was near to help or save. The skull was split open, both arms were broken, and other terrible injuries sustained. The tragedy must have taken place about ten a.m.; at two o'clock workmen there having noticed the horse grazing for some time from side to side of the road, with no one in charge, thought the circumstance suspicious and instituted a search, which resulted in the finding of the mangled remains in the valley below."[68]

Ross Valley can be seen over top of the Fort Amherst Lighthouse (Mary Ennis)

Captain Jackman and the Eagle Return from the Dead

There were no sailing vessels, only steamers, departing for the annual seal fishery from St. John's harbour in March 1887. The glory days of the sealing fleet was starting to decline when the following was penned;

> "The sealing fleet from this port, all steamers, took their departure on their adventurous voyage this morning. The *Eagle*, Captain Arthur Jackman, led the van at 5:30 o'clock, and was followed by the *Aurora*, Captain James Fairweather; which was succeeded by the *Neptune*, Captain Samuel Blandford, and the others passed out after each other in easy succession, all being gone in two hours afterwards. There was a marked absence the past ten days of the exciting stir and activity on the streets, which always accompanied in bygone times the preparations for this once great industry. The normal peace and quiet of the town was scarcely interrupted and if a stranger wasn't informed of the fact, he would never surmise that outfitting for the seal-fishery was going on and that twelve steamers, shipping crews aggregating some twenty-five hundred men, were being got in readiness. In the old days the spirits of men ran high and they showed in their demeanor what was in strong contrast to the half-heartedness and apathy that prevails to-day. The shopkeepers experienced no revival of business by the outfit for the sealfishery, and some say that they wouldn't know the sealers were getting to rights. Let us, however, hope for the best and trust that we may yet see a return to the use of sailing vessels by a wise and special encouragement to schooners. May the hardy men, who have just left us return laden deep with the spoils of frozen seas, and may their advent be a precursor of better times to Terra Nova."[69]

In spite of the gloomy article about the declining interest in the annual seal fishery, it was still an important event in the lives of the citizens of St. John's. The captains and ships were known by all and their movements followed like people follow their favorite sports team and players today. When several ladders were found on the ice belonging to the *Eagle* that Spring, rumor started building upon rumor in the city that something terrible must have befell the vessel. Soon people were believing that the well-liked Captain Jackman and his crew had become another tragedy of the sea. The wives and children of the sealers started to give up all hope of seeing their loved ones again and were ready to go into mourning. A cloud of doom seemed to hang over the city that Spring. On Easter morning as the church bells were ringing, summoning people to worship, a flag and ball were hoisted up on the flag staffs of the Block House signifying the approach of a sealer. The arrival of a sealer always evoked much interest in the townsfolk but this Spring the people were particularly interested and anxious about news on the *Eagle*. As word got around that it was the *Eagle*, almost as one the people responded;

> "...and from every quarter throngs poured down to Water Street, and on the piers and the road leading to the South Side was a moving stream of people.....From the moment that the staunch ship hove into view, throughout her course up the harbor she was followed by eager scrutinizing looks. She was "all there"........when..... the features of Captain Jackman and his men were once more discernable the pent-up emotions of the immense multitude, who covered docks, shipping and hill side, burst forth into a mighty cheering acclaim of welcome and congratulations. They were responded to by the thousands who lined the shore on this side, and back and forth across the harbor came and went the sounds of joy. Hundreds poured aboard the Eagle, and never was such a scene of handshaking and salutations witnessed in the history of the seal-fishery as then and there took place......"[70]

Captain Jackman and his crew were at once perplexed and flabbergasted at the response by the entire city it seemed on their homecoming. They had been unaware they were considered lost at sea and had entered the port expecting the usual few onlookers to greet them. It was a day none of them forgot for the rest of their lives.

The reported disaster was based upon the discovery of a few ship ladders on the ice which led to rumor and speculation that the ship and all the men were dead. Captain Jackman, still amazed at the turn of events on his arrival explained that the ladders had gotten tangled up in some ropes while a sail was being shifted and were thrown overboard. He also stated that he never had an easier time at the ice.

The *Eagle* had brought home 19,700 prime harps.

The seal hunt, c., 1880 (CNS)

Swept off the Rocks at the Fort Amherst Lighthouse

Three days after the *Eagle* had departed for the fishery on March 10, 1887, a local boy had a fatal accident on the ice;

> "Another unfortunate accident happened yesterday to impress upon the community the necessity of adopting safeguards to prevent boys of tender years bringing deadly risks upon themselves. The young lads living in the East End, about the Beach and Hoylestown, are particular prone to hazardous excursions over the ice, and in the present instance eight young lads belonging to this neighbor went out to the Narrows almost to the south headland where their ill-starred exploit had a disastrous ending. Their ages range from thirteen to fifteen, and they went out from the Queen's Wharf and landed on the other side, near Wareham's stage. Thence they went by the footpath toward Fort Amherst lighthouse, from the near vicinity of which steps used by the pilots and the lighthouse men, when the wind is offshore and boats can easily glide up the smooth beach of rock and stones. On this occasion the Easterly wind threw an immense surf into the place and approach to it would have been impossible - the waves would have flung their spray high up to the lighthouse - were it not that the ice subdued its violence, but it poured into the landing in huge rollers. The boys followed the wall of sea out some fifty feet, but ran back over the landwash before the next wave set inshore.They practiced those feats several times, one

Heavy seas near Fort Amherst Lighthouse (Joey Power)

trying to surpass the other in the distance he could pursue out the receding surf, when one of the boys, having recklessly ventured too far, was overtaken by the immense sea that, in returning to land, curled itself up twenty feet high. One or two of the others were also overtaken by the surf, but they clung with desperate strength to the rocks till the peril passed. They did not see their companion afterwards; for some time they looked, expecting that being a good swimmer he would struggle to shore, but the hope proved vain. They saw his cap floating on the surface and realising the worst, all knelt and prayed. The force of the surge had broken up the ice into small lumps and slob near the shore. Returning to town at once, they sought the police officer, but watchers on search last evening and this morning failed to find the body. The lost youth was Thomas Bolger, son of the late Mr. James Bolger, Water Street."[71]

Two More Melancholy Drownings

On Friday, November 25, 1887, the schooner *Ada Lake*, Captain Aaron Bennett, of Fortune, was inward bound when she struck and stranded on Pancake Rock. Three crewmen went out in a dory to drop a kedge anchor by which they planned to haul the craft off the rock. When they cast out the anchor, the boat upset and one of the men got entangled in the mooring rope and was carried to the bottom. The other two men swam to safety but the unfortunate victim never surfaced. The next day his companions went out searching for his body to no avail. The drowned man was a 23 year old native of Fortune Harbour, Fortune Bay named Percy. The craft was towed off the rock later and taken up the harbour.[72]

Something serious happened to Samuel Allan on April 28, 1888. He was a well known planter-fisherman of Black Head and left there that Saturday in his fishing boat for St. John's . He never returned home and his boat was later picked up by a schooner. *The Evening Telegram* adds more to the story;

"Present appearance bode ill for the discovery of Mr. Samuel Allan. Indeed all hope of finding him living is abandoned, and he is mourned as dead by his family. His son's place of business on Water Street West is closed. It would be a source of consolation to his family to have his body recovered, and with that object several boats' crews yesterday searched the water from Holwell's room in the Narrows, where he was last seen, outward, and also dragged the bottom with jiggers, but without avail. Amongst them was a boat manned by Mr. Thomas Grant, who examined the line of shore down to Quidi Vidi and searched the nooks in the cliff, but all to no purpose. The boat the lost man was in was a large fishing skiff; he was running under fore and main sails, alone, a common custom of his, and had a free wind from Blackhead to the Narrows, whence he was obliged to tack. It is supposed that in shifting the sheets he was tipped overboard. The tide runs out with the force and swiftness of a river through the narrow channel. Mr. Samuel Allan was one of those well known men whose name is synonymous with the settlement in which they live. The whole city knew him (he was about sixty-five years) and knew him favorably. He was a typical master-fisherman, intelligent, industrious and acquainted with every method of catching and curing all kinds of edible fish. He was a kind-hearted, hospitable man, and hosts of friends will sincerely grieve that his end was so sudden and tragic."

Samuel Allan's boat was picked up by a passing schooner a few days later but the man's disappearance remained another mystery of the sea.

Some 1888 Events

Safe passage through the Narrows depended on a lot of factors; wind, fog, ice, darkness. Many Springs saw the entrance blocked with ice and hundreds of crafts of all sizes trying to get either in or out. On May 9, 1888 when the ice went out, the boats came in;

"To-day's fresh wind from the westward set free the hundreds of boats hemmed in the neighboring harbors by the ice the past three weeks, and this forenoon the Narrows was blocked by them beating to and fro inward, as many as twenty-one having been counted there at one time, their barked sails obscuring the view out to sea. The sight is seldom seen in a lifetime. These boats are pretty nearly all from the Southern Shore, from Ferryland to St. Mary's. The coming week, and henceforth till the first week of next month, will be a busy time."[73]

A week after all the schooners scurried into port, the ice was back in blocking the Narrows. To add to the shipping woes on May 17th, a dense fog also enveloped the approach to the Narrows. The Allan steamer *Nova Scotia* was outside that Thursday firing signal guns. She was answered by the gun at Fort Amherst; the fog being so dense that the ship could be heard but not seen. The tug *D.P. Ingraham* was sent out to see what the ship wanted.

However, the ice eventually went out for good and by the first of June the local fishermen were bringing in some cod;

> "The first fresh cod of the season was sold here yesterday. To what fishermen the honor and glory belongs of catching this first fare is a point unsettled - some saying it was Mr. John Wareham, formerly of Raftus' stage, Riverhead, but now of Gunner's Cove, the Narrows; others aver that it was the Maher Brothers, the famous fish-killers of the West End. However that may be, the catchers got what was more tangible than honor and glory - fists-full of silver for the small quantities sold."[74]

For the second time in 1888, the little community of Black Head was struck with a tragedy. Three men named Power, a father, his son and his brother, left Job's wharf on Saturday evening, September 8th to return home to Black Head. They put out at 7 o'clock in a small punt with a barrel of flour on board. A strong westerly wind started to blow after they left the harbour. The next morning they still hadn't arrived. Two days later a boat supposed to be theirs, was picked up four miles off Cape Spear by a Bay Bulls craft.[75]

From R-L: Freshwater Bay (with iceberg), Deadman's Bay, Blackhead Bay and Cape Bay (Author)

Fort Amherst Criticized

Captain Craig of the steamer *Devonia* caused a slight controversy on March 3, 1889 when he accused the lighthouse keeper at Fort Amherst of not answering the steamer's guns. The ship with 150 passengers had left New York for Glasgow and had to come to St. John's due to a shortage of coal. They had a rough trip with blizzard conditions along the way and they ran into slob ice before they finally arrived off the harbour. The Cape Spear whistle helped guide them towards the mouth of the Narrows. The captain claimed he was unnecessarily detained there for two hours by the signalman at Fort Amherst who failed to answer his steamer's signals to give him a clue as to the lay of the land. Two days later, a letter to the editor signed "Eye-Witness,"stated that soon after the *Devonia* loomed up off the Narrows around 12:30, Sunday, a crew of pilots walked out to her on the ice from the area of Frederick's Battery as she was coming in. He then accused the pilots of not being on watch or they would have been out sooner. He saw them try to haul out a small boat but that didn't work. Eye-Witness figured the pilots should go outside the heads to ships instead of "crawling aboard ships inside of Chain Rock." The same day the letter appeared in print Austin Sheppard, the keeper at Fort Amherst, called at the office of *The Evening Telegram* and requested they deny the statement made by Captain Craig. He not only promptly responded to the *Devonia's* signals but sent his son, in great haste, to tell the tug-boat manager of the steamer's presence. The editor sided with Sheppard calling him a "faithful, and vigilant public servant." He also said that officers of ships are too apt to blame others for their own blunders. The agent for the steamer, Shea, gave her a quick dispatch and she left the same day.

Another Black Head Tragedy

In September 1889, an accident remarkably similar to one which had occurred almost exactly one year before, befell some more men of Black Head;

> "It is our painful duty to be again obliged to record a fatal accident to a Blackhead boat, homeward bound, yesterday evening, by which two men, of the

crew of three, lost their lives. In a rather small sized fishing boat, which was laden with a barrel of flour, the three men, Jeremiah Haley, aged 50 years, a widower with four children; Michael Murphy, his brother-in-law, aged 35 years, unmarried; and Thomas Murphy, aged 60 years, uncle to Michael, unmarried, left the premises of an east end firm at 4.30 o'clock. At the same time another Blackhead boat containing five or six men, and more deeply laden than the preceding with flour and provisions, started for home also, but when they reached the Narrows, observing the dangerous tumble of the sea produced by the fresh easterly wind, they decided to return to port. The other boat continued on. When off Long Point, about half a mile round the turn from the lighthouse, Jeremiah Haley, who was steering with an oar over the stern, leaned or pressed against the counter, the weather side being tilted considerably higher than the lee, when the counter gave way, the steering oar went overboard, the man lost his balance and fell into the sea. Poor Murphy, the younger, sprung to reach and save him, when he too, fell overboard. The third and only man now left in the boat is a cripple, and was unable to trim the sails, and so the only chance, short of swimming ashore, left the two men helplessly struggling with the waves, was lost to them. Deprived of her guidance of the helm, the sheets snapped off and the craft drifted onward, but directly toward her destruction. Those expecting her were looking out, and descried her in the condition mentioned. They boarded her and were appalled by the news told by the sole survivor. All the parties are well known here and bore the best of reputations as industrious fishermen and honest men."[76]

Michael Cantwell, one of the signalmen at the Block House on Signal Hill saw the terrible drama unfold before his eyes. He immediately notified the steam tugs who hastened to the scene. Cantwell hoisted the colours for the tug *Favorite* which was towing a vessel to sea and was just beyond the Heads at the time. The men could not decipher the message as they had no code on board, so they kept on going. Then Cantwell phoned to get Thorburn & Grieve's launch which immediately started out but unfortunately mistook the direction of the accident. When the *Favorite* was returning, Cantwell partly descended the cliff and shouted down to the men and told them about the accident. The tug at once steamed to the spot but it was too late, the men had disappeared. If the *Favorite* had been able to read Cantwell's message on their way out, they could have saved the men as they kept afloat for half an hour.

A Stabbing Affray In The Narrows

On Tuesday evening, October 1, 1889, two Petty Harbour fishermen were proceeding home in their punt alone. They were just off the Northern Head of the Narrows when a dispute of some kind arose between them and they started to quarrel. One of the men, Peter Parrell, gave his ship mate a nasty cut on the head with some object in the boat. The yell made by the injured party was so loud that an incoming fishing boat heard it and took the Petty harbour boat in tow. They took them to Clift's Cove in St. John's and summoned the police. Parrell was put in jail to await the result of his companion's injury. Both men were intoxicated at the time.[77]

More Ice Tales

By 1890, there were many regulations attached to the Newfoundland seal fishery such as the date when the fishery would start each year and even the time of day when sailing and steam vessels were allowed to depart. On March 10, 1890, Captain Blandford sailed the *Neptune* out two hours before the prescribed time. When he returned from the hunt, he was penalized. It was another hard year for ice as the port was blocked and shipping was halted. In early February, the steamer *Miranda* was three days in the Narrows trying to get out. Vessels arriving had to moor at the edge of the ice until they could be towed in; there were four there on February 4th.

Also in March, the *Boston Herald* told of plans to tow icebergs from Newfoundland to New England to supply ice for consumers there. There would not have had any shortage if they had carried out that plan!

The Newfoundland Colonist had two ice related stories, one on February 6th; 1890,

> "Three small boys came near losing the "number of their mess" this morning. They were out on the ice, when a large piece broke loose, carrying them out to sea. They were seen from the South battery, and hooked ashore by the light-house men."

And on March 20th , this amusing story entitled "Practicing for the Ice" was penned;

> "....A novel sight was witnessed in a house in this neighborhood a few days since, just before the steamers went to the ice; nothing more or less than a father teaching his son (who has since gone to the ice with Captain Sam) how to kill, sculp, pan, tie up and haul aboard a seal. The son was going out for his first trip and as he had signed as 'a man,' it was necessary he should know *something* about the business. In order to practically illustrate the business, the 'Thomas Cat' of the establishment was procured and was sewed into a piece of brin. The father then proceeded to cut off the covering from the cat, in the manner of sculping a seal, the son looking on admiringly. During the process the operator regaled the open-mouthed boy with the hair-breath escapes he had when he went to the ice. He was just finished a story of how he had been four days on an iceberg without food or water - when the cat having been 'sculped', stuck her claws into his face and gave him a bad scratching. The language which ensued brought his better half from the next room, who, on taking in the scene exclaimed, "Why, John, you were never outside the Narrows in your life!"

The year 1890 ended on a stormy note as a hurricane blew on the night of December 1st . People were saying that it surpassed the gale of '46 and old people who could remember that terrible night, refused to go to bed, sitting up all night "in fear and trembling."

During that storm, the *Emmeline* was wrecked below the Fort Amherst lighthouse and local fishermen lost a lot of property.

> "Near Gunner's Cove. - The gale and high sea of Tuesday last carried away the flake and part of the stage of Mr. King, planter, near Gunner's Cove, and a quantity of ship's timber from Mr. Ryan, the shipwright's place, near by. Mr. Vinicombe states that he lost a lumber-boat from his room in the same neighborhood. Mr. John Wareham's room and flakes sustained no damage."[78]

The Sheppards at Fort Amherst

The light keepers at Fort Amherst and Cape Spear were often instrumental in adverting a tragedy due to their constant vigilance at their posts. Most of the time their work went unnoticed but once in a while they would be complimented for the valuable job they did. The Fort Amherst keeper got a compliment in March, 1891;

> "Fort Amherst's Friendly Signal. - Captain Goss, of the barquentine *May Cory*, desires us to return his thanks to Mr. Sheppard, the worthy keeper of Fort Amherst Lighthouse, for the timely signal he hung out, and by means of which a tug came to the vessel's assistance and towed her safely into port. The blockhouse was enveloped in fog at the time and couldn't descry the ship."[79]

Perhaps the 'rose' thrown at Sheppard by Captain Goss made for the 'brick' hurled at him earlier in March, 1889 by Captain Craig of the *Devonia* incident.

Sheppard won a prize in a contest run by the Fisheries Commission in 1890. The Commission offered a reward of money to people residing on the coast of Newfoundland who submitted the best record of wind, weather condition, temperature of the sea, movement of fish, etc. On April 12,1891, the executive committee awarded the first prize of $50.00 to Mr. Austin Sheppard, Fort Amherst.

The Sheppard family had a long history at the Fort Amherst Light Station. John Sheppard had started there in 1852. His son Austin Oke Sheppard had taken over from him in 1887. None of Austin's sons followed in that noble calling, however, Austin's grandson, Captain Robert Carl Sheppard did from 1924- 1938.

During the late 1890s, Austin Sheppard, had extra reason to watch the waterway as his son, Robert Austin Sheppard, and a son-in-law, Robert Wakeham were ship captains working for shipping companies in St. John's.

In December, 1891, Robert Austin Sheppard was made captain of S. March & Sons' barquentine, *Nelly*. Captain R. Sheppard often competed with his brother-in-law, Captain Wakeham in races across the Atlantic or to and from Brazil. Wakeham had married Austin Sheppard's daughter in September which caused The Evening Telegram to write on September 3, 1891;

> "Cupid Enthroned In a Fort. - The flagstaff at Fort Amherst is dressed in gaily coloured bunting to-day, in honor of a nuptial event to which one of the inmates of the light-house is a party."

Light keeper Austin Sheppard had another son John who drowned in 1903 while working on his brother's ship. Captain Robert Sheppard disappeared with all his crew in 1910 somewhere in the Atlantic Ocean.

[See Appendix 6]

Fort Amherst Lighthouse bedecked with flags, c., 1890 (Joey Power)

Lost in the Narrows

On the night of July 8, 1891 at around nine o'clock, the steamer *Falcon* was proceeding out the Narrows bound for Sydney for coals. Midway between Chain Rock and the Southern Head she ran down the small schooner *Wave*, which sank almost immediately. The schooner, a fore-and-after, about 20 tons was owned by Stephen Johnson of Northern Bay and was deeply laden with caplin. Skipper Johnson gave the details of the accident to *The Daily Colonist*;

> "We were on our way from Northern Bay, with a load of caplin on board to sell in St. John's. We had a fine time, and reached the Narrows about nine o'clock. There was a light air of wind blowing out and we beating in, going very slowly. When about half way across, between Pancake and the other side, we saw a steamer coming out, heading right for us. We hollowed with all our might to attract the attention of those on board, but it was of no use; whether they did not hear or did not heed us, we cannot say; but the steamer came right on, striking us amidships, on the starboard side. It was a good thing for us that it was a load of caplin we had on board, for the cargo being spongy, half-yielding quality, it prevented the steamer from going right through the schooner. It was not very dark at the time, for though it was past twilight the lights of the harbor and town, and the bright sky made it clear enough to see a vessel three hundred yards away. The men on board the steamer realized what was the matter pretty quickly after the collision, and backing the steamer some what they stopped her and got out a boat. Although we were pretty well frightened we managed to launch our own boat, and an attempt was made to throw some loose things about the deck into her, but we recognized the fact that she was settling down, and so jumped for the boat. The persons on board beside myself were Bernard Hogan and William Hogan, who constituted the crew, and Ellen Hogan and Mary Jane Butler, passengers. Ellen Hogan is a married woman and had with her an infant child about a year old. Southside men who heard our cries also put off to our rescue and it was in one of these boats that the women were placed and sent on shore. They were given shelter for the night by the good people over there and were kindly treated. We stayed by the boat hoping that her damage might not be so bad as we thought, and that she might remain afloat. But our hopes were soon dispelled, and in ten minutes the schooner went down........"[80]

The men then rowed up the harbour and reported to the police who took them in for the night and treated them kindly. The loss was a heavy one for the men as each one would have earned $15.00 per man for the caplin. Mrs. Hogan, who was on her way to Montreal with her child to join her husband had a greater loss. She had furniture and household items on board which all went down with the *Wave*. Johnson felt that the crew of the steamer should have seen them and he realized they all had a narrow escape and were very lucky to be alive.

On August 9, 1891, two vessels, coasters, were beating in the Narrows and crashed into each other. It could have been avoided if one had given way but both stubbornly held to their course. One reached port safely while the other drifted towards the Southern Head and a tug had to come to its assistance. Shortly after the collision, a shark appeared upon the scene and was clearly seen as it broke water. Luckily, no one fell into the water at that time. However, the editor warned, "Beware, ye Chain Rock bathers, of the whales and the man-eating shark!"[81]

In September, another steamer and schooner met in the Narrows with a predictable result. However, this time the steamer came out the worse of the confrontation. The steamer *Coban* arrived at the entrance from Montreal. While coming in, an outport schooner beating out tacked right under the steamer's bow forcing her to run nearer the shore than she normally would. A collision was thus avoided but the ship struck on the Pancake Rock, sliding up on the rock a foot or two. The engines were reversed but the vessel held fast. It was dead calm at the time and the tide was low. The tug *Ingraham* went out and tried to tow her off but the *Coban* wouldn't budge. Police officers and Customs officers also went on board to be prepared for any emergency in the event of a wreck. They waited for the high tide and then they towed her off and steamed up to her pier at Harvey & Co. Surprisingly, there was no damage done to the vessel.[82]

Two Quidi Vidi Accidents

A Quidi Vidi man and his sons had a frightening experience on September 23, 1891;

> "A skiff belonging to Quidi Vidi, and manned by Skipper Young and his sons, got caught in the northeast gale last night, and had a narrow escape; but the Skipper managed to land one of his sons at Hay Cove, and at nine o'clock the latter appealed to the pilots for help. The crew of No. 1 Boat gallantly responded,

> and, in the teeth of the gale, pulled out through the Narrows and effected a rescue. The skiff's sails were blown to pieces, and she was drifting towards the breakers when the pilots took hold of her. The names of No. 1 Boat, Samuel Ryan, John Eagan, Richard Vinicombe, and Peter Hannon, members of the crew."[83]

On October 14, 1891, three men were returning from squidding and had a narrow escape from drowning outside Quidi Vidi. William Mitchell, Garrett Pendergast and son were entering the gut as the entrance is called, in a heavy sea. The very narrow opening is difficult to approach in a calm sea and nearly impossible when the sea is breaking across the entrance. As they entered, their boat was pitched upon a rock and smashed to pieces and all the occupants were hurled into the wild sea. They would have certainly drowned except for the quick assistance of Thomas Burton who preceded them a short distance away. Burton returned and had great difficulty in rescuing the men. William Mitchell sank twice before he could be hauled aboard the boat.[84]

In contrast to the last scene, *The Evening Telegram* wrote this article on November 10, 1891;

> "A Pen-Picture In the Narrows To-Day. - A pleasing view might have been obtained by looking towards the Narrows this morning at sunrise. A favorable change of wind having taken place during the night, a great number of sailing craft seized the opportunity to start for the different ports. It would almost seem as if daylight had been agreed upon as a signal for sailing simultaneously, as at that time a fleet of about twenty ships came down the harbor in a body, with all sail set, and, as they approached the Narrows, massed themselves together as a cloud of canvas. A dim haze enveloped them and gave a fantastic appearance to the picture, as the sun, rising like a red ball of fire, cast across them its lurid rays of light. Gradually the schooners edged their way to the open bay, avoiding collision with considerable skill, and, as they reached into the swell of the Atlantic, dipped themselves gracefully as a morning salute to Neptune, and then, spreading themselves as birds on the wing, shaped their course for their different destinations. Beautiful as the picture was from as outside point of view, we can imagine it will be still more beautiful (in a different sense) in the eyes of the wives and children of the men on board the different schooners as the latter approach their harbours, and gladden the hearts of the former by the return of their bread-winners with a supply of provisions to tide them over the coming winter."

A Terrifying Experience

The biggest news that in the Spring of 1892 was the wreck of the schooner *Pointer*. It was another frightening story of a near tragedy in the Narrows;

> "The schooner *Pointer*, of about forty tons, Michael McLoughlin, master, owned by Messrs. McCormack & Walsh, of Catalina, whilst on her way from Catalina to this port, in ballast, capsized out in the Narrows before 10 o'clock this forenoon. She was sailing towards Freshwater Bay, and when to the windward of the large iceberg off the South Head of the Narrows, a squall broke upon her. She greatly careened, the ballast shifted and she capsized. Those on board had to scramble for their lives, and narrowly escaped. The boat which, very fortunately, was held by tackle, swung nicely over on the foresail, and, after a time, all were got into it. Those on board the schooner were: Mr. Nicholas Walsh, part owner, Michael McLoughlin, master, Joseph Gullage, William Nowlan, and two passengers - Thomas and Susannah Way, brother and sister. In the struggle for life Mr. Walsh had his side injured. Miss Way was in the cabin at the time of the accident, and the master reached his hand down the skylight, caught her, and hauled her out on deck. Just as he did so the water went gushing into the cabin. Afterwards, as Miss Way stood on one of the sails, she sank to her waist in water, and one of the men went down to his neck in getting to her to render assistance. In the meantime, the schooner *Pet*, Joyce, master, coming from Clode Sound, sailed towards her, and, when in a line with the Narrows, ran a flag at half mast, and almost at the same time, two guns were fired from the South Battery. Shortly afterwards, the tug *Favorite* steamed to the *Pointer* and took her in tow; and in a little while the *D.P. Ingraham* appeared on the scene. When the schooner was towed within two hundred yards of the Narrows, she sank beneath the surface, an an order to cut the tow line was given, but immediately countermanded. It was decided to hold her the longest possible time. Entering the Narrows, however, the tow line broke, it is thought by the schooner striking the Merlin Rock, and, the schooner sank to the bottom. She is now in the centre of the Narrows, near Chain Rock, with her topmast over water. Mr. Walsh is making arrangements to have a diver go down to fasten a rope to her spars and a tug to raise her a little and tow her in. The young woman and her brother seemed dazed this forenoon from fright. The former was nervous and a little chilled; but under the care of Mrs. Walsh, with whom she resides at present she will soon be her normal state. Life is precious; they saved that."[85]

The Pointer was coming to St. John's to buy supplies at Bowring Bros. Early next morning, Thursday, June 3rd, a throng of small boats were hovering around the mast of the *Pointer* still sticking up out of the water. Many eyes had watched the drama unfold in the Narrows the day before and now were out looking for salvage. Browing Bros.' regular diver was out of town so they procured the diver of the H.M.S. *Emerald* who went down and examined the wreck. He reported little damage done and it would not be too difficult to raise her; a great expense for the owners as the $1,500.00 vessel was not insured. On Friday they got the schooner up in this manner;

> ".....A schooner, the *Ivanhoe*, was brought near her, two lengths of steel cable were run, one each, through the hawse-holes, then down and fastened to each side of the stern of the *Pointer*. Turns of it were taken around the *Ivanhoe's* windlass, which was hove upon till the *Pointer* was considerably raised. Meanwhile, other steel cables were run down and one each put through the *Pointer's* hawse-holes and made fast. The tug *D.P. Ingraham* then came along, took on board both ends of these cables, set them tight, just by hand, and steamed ahead. The towage strain sufficiently raised the *Pointer* to clear her of bottom, and away all went to the south wharf of the dry dock, where the schooner now is awaiting turn to go on the dock. It was rather novel to have a vessel with all canvas set sailing beneath the surface of the water."[86]

A schooner passes Chain Rock (MHA)

A Line Across The Narrows

A 'first' for the Narrows occurred in June, 1892. St. John's was all abustle with preparations for the return of Monsignor Michael Howley who was to be consecrated as the first Newfoundland born bishop of a Newfoundland diocese on June 24th. To welcome home the Monseignor and his distinguished party, it was decided to string a line 300 feet high, across the Narrows with the words, "Welcome Our Distinguished Countryman," in six feet high letters. The project was undertaken by Mr. F. J.Kenny who had men working on both sides of the Narrows by June 20nd, two days before the *Nova Scotian* was to arrive with the Monsignor. The idea of a line across the Narrows was first looked upon as impossible and "chimerical," but Kenny disproved that opinion when he succeeded. He used seven coils of three inch manila rope supplied by J. H. Monroe of the Rope Walk (an industrial area now known as Ropewalk Lane). The coils amounted to 2,700 feet of rope! Men mounted a windlass and other mechanical devices up by the Queen's Battery on Signal Hill and similar plans were carried out on the corresponding height on the South Side Hill. On June 22nd, the steamer arrived early sending everyone in a flutter. The letters may not have been up at that time because it was too windy to put them up the day they were stringing the rope across and Kenny decided to wait until Consecration Day. Two weeks later, the schooner *Canford* had its maintopsail carried away by the rope which had dried and drooped low across the Narrows.

The editor of *The Evening Telegram* must have been short of items for his paper on July 6th 1892, for he could have penned the following account in about three lines;

> "An 'ancient and brave' fisherman of the Southside and two of his sons left their homes on Sunday night to sail for the fishing grounds in Freshwater Bay. The breezes blew and the billows rolled, and the 'ancient and brave' returned not; neither did the young men. Family and friends feared their fate. Last night, suffering souls yearned for sympathy and were given it abundantly; perhaps too abundantly. 'Poor William and the boys are gone!' But, no! 'Fine night,' said the watchman in his first call, 'and good tidings,' added a jubilant voice. 'Here comes William and the boys!' Quickly did a few persons proclaim the glad news. Out turned half the Southside people, and away with them to the

dock wharf to greet William and the boys, returning, not dead, but alive and with a boat load of fish. Didn't they greet them, didn't they question them, and didn't they surprise *them*! - Where had they been? Well, they just ran into Blackhead out of the breeze and the billows, and occupied some of their time working in a potato garden. For this kindness they were *baited*, and upon the baiting they loaded.You see reader, there may always be a reasonable hope from the ocean or - the potato garden."

Things weren't so funny on July 8, 1892, when a terrible fire destroyed a great part of St. John's including *The Evening Telegram* office. The paper was out of circulation until the last day of August. Some ships escaped destruction by sailing out through the Narrows on that terrible day and night. In the following weeks, many relief supply ships entered port and with the unanimous consent of all the pilots, C. Lewis piloted the steamer *Newfield* in, free of charge with supplies on August 4, 1892.

Looking west at St. John's after 1892 fire (PANL)

Two and a half weeks after the great fire, a sad drowning took place off the Narrows. A small boat was on her way to Placentia Bay when crewman Willis Collins of Flat Islands was knocked overboard by the mainboom. He drowned before his shipmates could reach him; he was only 15 years old.[87]

1893: A Busy Year

The Year 1893 saw a lot of incidents in the Narrows with vessels hitting the rocks, being driven out to sea, etc., [see appendix 4]. A near tragedy occurred in Freshwater Bay on August 31, 1893;

> "Three men named Thomas Branville, Richard Branville and Michael Forristal, who went out fishing in Freshwater Bay yesterday, were very near remaining there for ever, or at least, until the sea would give up its dead, and they would have done so were it not that a boat owned by Mr. Bennett of the Southside happened to be near at the time of the accident which occurred by an extra heavy squall of wind striking Branville's boat broadside, and, notwithstanding the ballast and fish, capsized her. It was with immense difficulty that the men clambered to the keel. When the men in Bennett's skiff saw the accident, they made good speed to the upturned boat; and took the crew up, cold and tired, and brought them to the lighthouse, where, through the kindness of Mr. Sheppard, they were made comfortable and had a good dinner. If Bennett's boat had not seen the accident, the lives of those men would have been lost, and, death in a terrible manner would have been their portion.......All the fish and the boat herself have now either gone to the bottom or miles out to sea.......truly a fisherman's calling is no sinecure......."[88]

Loss of the Martin Luther

Fortunately, in all the incidents previously mentioned in 1893 there was no loss of life. That changed with the loss of the *Martin Luther* near Wash Balls on Sunday night, October 15th;

> "Last night another maritime casualty on our coast was added to the already long list, by the total wreck, near Wash Balls, of the Norwegian wood-barque Martin Luther, Captain S. Stensen......She left Mathil, Scotland, for Sydney, to receive orders, which were to proceed to St. John's to take on board the deal cargo of the wrecked barque *Martha*, condemned here. She is a heavy

ship and left Sydney at 5 o'clock on last Monday evening......a good run, for a strange captain, was made last night for the Narrows.....The very mouth of the Narrows was made shortly after 9 o'clock, and then the baffling wind and strong current tending the vessel toward the point of the Northern Head, an anchor and about 19 fathoms of cable were let go, but did not hold her......flare ups.....were ignited to summon help.....Soon the vessel fell in against the cliff between the Northern Head and Wash Balls, her bows towards the Fort Amherst Lighthouse, and a mad scramble for life was made amidst surging and thundering seas against the rock-bound coast......One of the large boats was being lowered, an eager rush was made to get into it......When six men had taken place, the stern ring-bolt and the wood to which it was fastened went clear, with the unfortunate result that the stern of the boat falling quickly down, bringing the boat almost perpendicular, the two men in the stern were precipitated with velocity into the seething waters and drowned. They floated along rapidly by the side of the vessel; one of them was heard to give his last agonizing shriek before entering the portals of eternity......Five or six life lines and one life buoy were thrown without avail. The two were: Karl Gooth, aged 19 years, single, and able to swim, and Andreas Nikolaison, aged 21 years, married, and unable to swim; both heavily clothed. They belonged to Norway. The four in the boat now tried to rescue their shipmates from the wrecked vessel. Their attempt was not effectual. Then they pulled frantically for shore, for life and for help - breaking two oars as they did so. In the Narrows they were met by a pilot boat manned by Mr. John Gallishaw, assisted by Messrs. William Cantwell, James Collins and William Lewis. The pilot crew ordered the wrecked ones to proceed on their way to shore; they meanwhile going to the lighthouse to despatch word up to the dock for the *Favorite*.....The tug left at 11:30, but could not do anything, failing to find a vestige of the vessel in the darkness. The pilot boat, however...... had been in touch with the *Aureola*, nearing the wreck, the crew dropped her grapnel, paid out sixty fathoms cable, and got a line to the vessel, and a man to work each rope. During the lulls the boat was pulled into the side of the vessel, one of the crew would run down the ladder, hustle on board, and then the boat was pulled clear again with all strength and speed. Thus it continued till the eight were in the boat. The crew all counted, numbered fourteen........The vessel hove over on her side, spars out from the land, and has been badly battered up, a hopeless wreck......"[89]

The twelve survivors were sheltered at the Police Station that night and next day taken to the Seaman's Home. More information was given about the *Martin Luther* disaster the next day. The ship first sighted Fort Amherst light at 6 o'clock on Sunday evening. There was neither a tug nor pilot on the scene so the captain decided to venture in alone rather than remain outside in the storm. Good work was done by the lighthouse men, who fired several guns to hurry the rescuers along. The sailors lost all their belongings and while two men drowned, two dogs on board jumped into one of the boats and were saved.

The men went out to the wreck the next day and looked for their drowned shipmates but they were not found. There were many local boats at the wreck salvaging sails, spars, etc.

One of the spars of the wrecked vessel was still sticking out towards the middle of the Narrows in mid November. Even a year later in August, the spar was still visible above the sea by the Northern Head.

In November, 1893 there were two more serious mishaps in as many days in the Narrows. The first was on Friday the seventeenth;

> "This morning, about 11.30, the little schooner *Annie*, belonging to Messrs. Thorburn & Tessier and in charge of Captain John Blundon of Bay-de-Verde, while attempting to beat in the Narrows suffered serious damage. She was 'hauling up' to get out of the way of another craft and the strain being very great the main stay broke followed by the foresail splitting through the middle and bursting away from the gaff. The men did their utmost to keep their craft off, but slowly she drifted ashore and struck the rocks on the Northern side of the Narrows, near Chain Rock. Two of the men instantly jumped ashore and the sea brought the craft off again, but almost instantly dashed her back against the rocks; this time the mate, taking a girl, daughter of the captain, with him, jumped ashore and leaving the girl on the rocks regained the vessel, though, not without some injury to himself. The craft struck the rock some five or six times more and then a tug, in answer to repeated calls, came and took her and all the crew off. The tug brought the *Annie* up to Messrs. Thorburn & Tessier's wharf, aided by a number of men on the wharf with ropes. She was hauled in and instantly sank. When the *Annie* struck she had on board the whole product of the men's earnings, all of which is destroyed. The season's fishery was not big but its fruit was on board. The names of the crew are: John Blundon, master, John Hennessey, second hand (this man was very much injured while jumping ashore with the daughter of the master), John Power and Patrick Walsh. The *Annie* now lies on bottom at Thornburn & Tessier's wharf, and the men, with boat-hooks, are taking up clothing, etc., from the hold."[90]

In the same paper the next day was this account of another mishap;

> "Another Schooner Ashore - *Hannah G.*, 46 tons, Doyle of King's cove, master, from Gambo, consigned to the Messrs. Sclater with a cargo of lumber. In beating in the Narrows, about 9 o'clock last night, she misstayed inside the Southern Head and went ashore on the rocks in a cove just inside the Fort Amherst lighthouse, and is in a good way to become a total wreck."

The tug *D.P.Ingraham* towed the *Hannah G.* off the rocks at 4:30 that same day and into the harbour.

Snatched from the Jaws of Death

The year 1893 had been a rough one for shipping around St. John's. Many vessels had difficulty getting safely out or in through the Narrows. Also, many vessels en route to St. John's were not always able to gain the Narrows. An example of the difficulty in sea travel in the days of sail was reported in *The Evening Telegram,* December 18, 1893.

The year ended on a rough note at least for two crafts in mid December. One craft had departed Ferryland for St. John's with six people by the names of Kehoe, Curran, Boland, Quirk, a passenger (no name given) and Henry White on board. A storm soon came on and the vessel was driven out to sea. The men saw another craft, the *Pixie*, also in trouble and they signalled each other. In the meantime, word was given to the tug *Ingraham* to go out and search for the missing vessels which she did. The tug returned after searching unsuccessfully for the vessels. Meanwhile, fifty miles off Cape Spear a high seas drama was unfolding as the two battered crafts maneuvered near to each other. After comparing notes it was decided that Kehoe's ship was worst and so the people transferred to the *Pixie*. They had made the right choice because Kehoe's craft sank with all the fish and gear; they only saved a bit of clothing. When they finally reached the Narrows, there was no tug out so they had to put two anchors out and wait until the *Favorite* took them in. They had used up all their coal and had very little water left and if they had been driven out to sea again, the result would have been much worse if not fatal.

A ship in trouble at sea (Joey Power)

Never a Dull Moment

On March 26, 1894 the Fort Amherst fog gun was booming at the battery there and in the harbour a whistle was blowing causing everyone to wonder what was the matter. Some thought it was a sealer coming home from the seal fishery. The reason for all the racket was;

> "Yesterday Messrs.Thomas Shortall, Thomas Allan, Thos. Grant, Angel and others - three Toms and an Angel - went out on a pleasure and sealing cruise in Angel's steam launch. The launch broke down under them, and, during the height of the storm drifted helplessly on the bosom of the turbulent sea........Something had to be done. That something was done by Mr. Allan, a Blackhead man, who knows the bay well. He took to the dingy, braving the storm, made land and procured the aid of the 'D.P. Ingraham,' which sailed at about 9 o'clock and returned an hour later.......Mr. Green speaks to-day in indignant terms about having to get steam up to go out, and seems like as if he would wish some person to pay up handsomely."[91]

Exactly one week before that incident, the *Portia* had arrived at the Narrows late at night in a heavy snow fall. Captain Ash had difficulty in seeing the entrance and it was only by the frequent firing of the gun by the light keeper, he was able to get his bearings and enter safely. The next day, Captain Ash wrote a thank-you to the keeper at Fort Amherst in a local paper for "the flashes of a few guns at the South Battery."

During the Spring of 1894, a lot of local people were going outside the Narrows to hunt a few seals. On Saturday, March 25th, the ice came in tight to the land and several parties went off looking for seals. A Blackhead punt brought in eight, the tug *Ingraham* got a few, the *S.S.Virginia Lake*, and *Jenny Foote* went out cruising "for seals and for pleasure." All this sealing activity caused one observer to quip, "Long ago the steamers used to go north to get the seals, and now the seals come south to get the steamers."

Captain Blanford in Job's *Neptune* had a poor catch that Spring causing him to remark to one of his crew while still at the ice, "I have only a few more days to live; when I get ashore Mr. Job will hang me!"

The Evening Telegram wrote about, 'The Pilot's Plucky Feat' On October 4, 1894;

> "The boarding of the *Corean*, nearly three miles outside the Narrows, yesterday, by Mr. Charles Lewis, was, indeed, a plucky feat. Repeatedly went the boat away up on the crested foam, and down in the tough of the sea, now threatened with being swept out of the water, and again threatened with an instant submerging. The steamer had been hove to, and when the boat succeeded in getting within twenty yards of her she had to be hove to also, death seeming imminent. A fresh effort was, however, made, it was death or glory, and glory won. The ship was boarded and brought safely into port. The crew, too, deserve full mead of praise. The boat is a staunch and buoyant one, the Elizabeth, formerly owned by Mr. Lewis' father, an ancient pilot, and was at one time a successful race boat on Quidi Vidi lake. Our pilots, in their comparatively small boats, are truly plucky men. They recognize 'danger on the deep,' experience and brave it."

A Benign Year

There were no serious accidents or deaths in and around the Narrows in 1895 but there was plenty of activity. After the sealing fleet left in March it was noted that there was only one sailing vessel, the *Portland*, Jackman master, departing St. John's that year. The rest of the fleet was steam driven causing one person to lament, "What a difference from the glorious days when vessels filled a channel from Maggotty Cove to Riverhead," and "Oh, for the return of the good old days of the sailing vessels! Steam has been the bane of the sealing industry. They are expensive toys, the sooner they disappear and give place to the old time sailing vessels the better."

That year was one of the most successful sealing voyages on record, nearly half a million dollars earned in six weeks. The sealing steamer, *Aurora*, Jackman, locked the doors of the icefield when he was the last one back on May 9, 1895. They brought back an enormous walrus weighing nearly half a ton which had been shot from the bow of the steamer by Captain Jackman. It became the object of sight-seeing jaunts for the citizens of the city as they traveled to Bowring's wharf on the Southside to view it..

As was the case most summers, fishermen were in the local news quite frequently. The summer of 1895 saw a lot of local and outport men fishing out of St. John's which led to a lot of traffic in and outside the Narrows. On July 20th , there were "scores of fishing boats sailing in the Narrows." Off Cape Spear on the ledge known as 'Old Harry', William

Carter caught a codfish weighing 48 ½ pounds.

On July 12th, the attention of *The Evening Telegram* was turned to other activities out in the bay;

> "There were many boating parties, many ladies, outside the Narrows yesterday afternoon, enjoying an easy pull on the tranquil waters. There was quite a large party at the same time, near Fort Amherst lighthouse, dancing on the green, and participating in general exhilaration."

There was one close call outside the Narrows for a young man on Saturday, October 5, 1895;

> "A young man in a boat out in the Bay on Saturday evening was daring enough to run for and board the *Hope*, being towed at a rate of ten knots an hour. He ran close by all right, fended off with great difficulty, and cast the end of his long line on board. While he was arranging matters the line was paid out just sufficiently for his boat to go in the wash of waters at the stern of the vessel, and so fall in right across the rudder, one gunwale going under, and water pouring into the boat. 'Hold on and steer!' was shouted. 'Hold on and save yourself!' seemed more applicable at the time. However, the boat was steered, ran out clear, straightened up, the tow-line hauled in, the swamping averted, and 'Davy Jones' Locker' cheated of an inmate."[92]

Alluding to that incident, the same paper said that the *Hope* came in without a pilot Saturday afternoon. "The tug did part of the work and an amateur boarded her outside of Chain Rock, but he will get no fare."

A Death on the Ice

The year 1896 would not prove as benign as the previous year. The ice blocked the coast and 136 icebergs were visible from Signal Hill. With the ice came the seals and parties of men went out to hunt them leading to a tragedy on April10, 1896.

Hundreds of seals were killed that day but the unpredictable ice started to loosen and the men and boys had to hurry to land, many leaving their catch behind. Three men from St. John's, however, got caught out on the drifting ice all night. James Sullivan left the city in the morning with a friend named Squires who returned when he got his seals. Sullivan went out off Cape Spear about two miles and got a tow of 'fat' which he

Men and ships on ice in Narrows, c., 1890. Gunner's Cove in background. (CNS)

subsequently had to 'slip' (leave). Patrick Barron and James Billings also went out together early in the morning. They procured their seals beyond the cape. At 2:00 Billings fell in the water near the bill of the cape and Barron rescued him with great difficulty. Although Barron could have landed on the cape at that point, he would not leave his friend who was greatly weakened and traumatized by his immersion in the icy water. By 4:00 p.m. the two men were near Sullivan and all three were drifting south pass the cape, weary and hunger. They finished their meagre supply of food and Sullivan ate a seal heart to try and strengthen himself. As they drifted pass Petty Harbour, no boat came out to their rescue; Billings gave up hope and shortly after, he died. Barron was now left alone with his dead friend as Sullivan was a distance away. But help was on the way as the lighthouse keeper at Cape Spear had reported their plight to St. John's. The *Virginia Lake* had pulled into Bay Bulls and when Captain Taylor was informed, he immediately set of to the rescue. The men and the corpse were taken to their anxious relatives in St. John's. As the men sadly related their ordeal, Barron said, "The hardest part on me now is to tell Billings's wife of the death."[93]

Pandemonium in the Narrows!

Every year when the hundreds of outport crafts flocked to St. John's for supplies and to sell their fish, there were always a few mishaps in the Narrows. But in June 1896, there seemed to be an exceptionally high number of accidents. *The Evening Telegram* for June is full of the activity In the Narrows. On June 1st, there were over twenty vessels of the local fleet mentioned and several accredited the men at Fort Amherst with their safe entry. During the fog, the gun at the lighthouse answered every gun fired by a vessel outside. One schooner entering, collided with the barquentine, *Electra* doing a little damage to the latter. Further damage was averted by the schooner quickly dropping her anchor which halted her headway.

On the second day of June, the schooner *Bloomingdale* went on the rocks. She was charted by John Score to sail with a cargo of limestone and left early on a fresh southwest breeze. All went well as she clipped smartly down the harbour but when she entered the narrow channel, the winds were baffling, coming down off the hills. The crew had a difficult time handling the vessel and when nearly outside, she became unmanageable and drifted in on the shore. The rudder was lost and other damage was sustained as she pounded on the rocks. Bowring Bros. steam launch was outside and hastened to her rescue and towed her off the rocks. Only for the quick rescue, the *Bloomingdale* would have been a total wreck.

On the fourth, there were about forty schooners in the Narrows at 1:30 p.m. Some were becalmed dangerously near the rocks and the tugs had a busy time towing them in; one steam launch had three in tow at one time. One schooner went ashore and "there were some good sporting to get her off."

The calm weather mentioned above must have been the calm before the storm for the paper next day was full of accidents. When the S. S. *Polina* reached the Narrows at 11:00 p.m., she was unable to get in because the Narrows was blocked with vessels of all kinds. They were so thickly anchored across that they were described as being arranged as 'so many walls of Troy.' Captain Lechance plowed into the schooners before he realized the situation and a main boom of one schooner was struck. He backed the *Polina* out and had to stay outside all night.

The Royal Gazette on June 9, 1896, quoting *The Evening Herald* of June 5th, gave the reason for the blockage in the Narrows;

> "Rarely, if ever, was such a spectacle presented as that of the Narrows and offing yesterday afternoon. The free wind brought hundreds of northern crafts along, and as they bore up for the entrance the iceberg near Chain Rock barred the way, and the baffling squalls made it very dangerous for them to attempt entering. They anchored and as others followed in great numbers these had to follow suit, until a fleet of crafts of various sizes filled the offing. Many of these were in danger of getting hove ashore by the seas, collisions were momentarily occurring, and few escaped damage. The tugs had a rich harvest towing two and sometimes three at a time, and continued at it until dark, but fully 100 vessels had to remain there all night. These were in great danger, owing to the tremendous sea and very few of the crews slept, all anxiously watching and trying to keep their crafts from damage. The thunderous sound made as they met in rolling, could be heard along the shore, and it is a great wonder more damage was not done. Lines that were run out snapped like threads in the strain, and a few were found to let go a second anchor, while the movements of icebergs were keenly watched by all."

In *The Evening Telegram* next day, there was over 65 entries under 'Our Local Fleet' column. A lot of them had been damaged during the pandemonium the night before. Some of the damages were:

> *Spinaway*, Howell, about $40.00 worth of damage done in the Narrows
> *Caber Faigh*, Sheppard, Harbor Grace, damaged the stem while in the Narrows
> *Henietta*, James Oldford, Goose Bay, lost two anchors and one chain
> *Ellen,* W. Butt, Western Bay, 17 passengers, there was good crew to work her in the emergency that occurred
> *Enterprise*, W. Payne, Brookfield, carried away main boom and head gear in the Narrows, etc.

The schooner *Annie*, Bussey, master from Random, had to be abandoned. She was run into by another craft which set her foremast swinging loosely about and she became leaky. The crew abandoned the vessel and left her anchored in the Narrows.

The *Eugene Prince*, John Prince, from Southern Bay fell over on the iceberg in the Narrows while under full sail and had a lot of damage done to her hull.

Some schooners couldn't fit inside the crowded Narrows and had to anchor outside all night. The *Lizzie R.*, White, from Greenspond anchored in 27 fathoms of water and held on until daylight.

Another vessel wasn't so lucky;

> "There was an exciting event out in Freshwater Bay last night, and a desperate struggle for life and for safety from a watery grave. The *White Squall*, G. Penny, master, arrived thus far from Western Bay, C.B., in ballast. At 11:30 o'clock at night she drove close in to the land, between Black Head and Cape Spear. She soon went in among the breakers, getting hard knocks. Matters turned out so suddenly that there was not even an anchor dropped. There was a wild scramble for life. The nine men and one woman on board jumped into the boat - an old one that you would hardly cross to the Southside under ordinary circumstances - bringing some effects with them. They then, with only two oars at their command, pulled for St. John's, arriving here at 2 a.m."[94]

The *White Squall* eventually went ashore at Seal Cove about six miles beyond Renews on the Southern Shore.

The day after the big pile up in the Narrows, the crews of those vessels were complaining loudly to the authorities because no help had been given them in their perilous condition. However, pilots Ryan, Gallishaw, Eagan and two assistants were out there that night, moving about among the crafts, running out lines and helping in various ways. As the paper noted, much more damage would have been done, perhaps lives lose if the men of No.1 pilot boat had not been there, "Well done, brave pilots!" The paper also wrote that now there was a big job for any interested party to "fish up anchors, chains, etc., from the bottom, in and about the Narrows."

There were many more incidents in the Narrows that year. [See Appendix 4] Most were the usual groundings on the rocks which littered the channel.

In August, someone finally realized that a buoy should be placed on Cahill's Rock;

> "Mishaps are so frequent at Cahill's Rock, in the Narrows, that the placing of buoy over it seems very necessary. The opinion appears to be that it's all right for foreigners coming here who have pilots on board, but not so for the hundreds of our own vessels sailing in and out, and particularly when beating against head winds. It is admitted that most of the skippers have a knowledge of the existence of the rock, and even a general knowledge of its location, but not sufficient knowledge to avert danger."[95]

On Thursday, October 15, 1896, a captain nearly lost his life in the Narrows;

> "The schooner *William*, J. Balsam, master, from Random, T.B., received damage at 1 o'clock this morning which nearly proved disastrous to life. While in the Narrows she was struck by a severe squall and thrown over almost on her beam ends by a heavy sea at the same time. The mainsail was struck with great force, and when it jibbed it carried away the sheet iron and that part of the rail to which it was attached. The iron tiller was also worked off the rudder-head. The master of the vessel stood at his post of duty right in the midst of all the wreckage. How he avoided having his head knocked off and his body hurled overboard seems a puzzle to the crew. The vessel arrived in port under difficulties. The crew puts it this thus, 'We just got in and saved our lives.' "[96]

Two weeks later in October, the following collision occurred;

"The *Jessie*, Howell, master, sailed at six o'clock on Saturday evening for Catalina, taking as passengers Capt. William Rodgers and the crew of the banking schooner *Charlie F. Mayo*. When out in the Narrows the steam-tug *Favorite*, taking in the barquentine *Fanny* and the brigantine *May*, was met, and a collision occurred. There was quite a heavy shock felt on board the *Jessie*, which vessel had some of her head gear carried away, and Capt. Rodgers jumped over her side and got on board the *Fanny*, which vessel brought him into port. The *Favorite* was afterwards sent out in search of the *Jessie*, but the vessel could not be located. It is presumed that she sailed on her way." [97]

Lots of traffic in the Narrows, c., 1890 (City of St. John's Archives)

Thirteen Lives Lost: The Tiber and Maggie Tragedy

The year 1896 had been a terrible one for accidents and near misses in and around the Narrows. Fortunately, since the death of the sealer Billings in the Spring, no more lives had been lost. But all that changed on Friday night, November 6, 1896 when the *Tiber* and *Maggie* collided with tragic results. The S.S.*Tiber*, Captain J. Delisle, left Shea's wharf at 7:00 p.m., pilot Richard Vinicombe left her around Chain rock and the vessel proceeded on her way to Montreal. Meanwhile, the 57 ton schooner *Maggie*, owned and commanded by Captain William Blundon was making her approach to the Narrows. The *Maggie* had left Brooklyn,

Goose Bay in Bonavista Bay on Thursday morning with a cargo of 1000 quintals of fish for St. John's. She had 23 people on board, 9 crew and 14 passengers. The captain's wife who seldom came to the city, was induced to do so because she was bringing her invalid son Levi along to get medical attention in St. John's. Although the evening was dark, the weather was fine and all were looking forward to getting on shore in less than an hour and perhaps take in some of the sights of Water Street before the shop lights were turned off.

The schooner passed the Narrows in the offing and went into Freshwater Bay a ways before coming around for the entrance. She had both her lights burning as she came around near the Southern Head; James Power was at the wheel and some of the men were back aft paying out the main sheet. Meanwhile, the *Tiber* was nearing Chain rock and when her lights were noticed by the schooner, word was passed around that a steamer was coming out and to watch out for her. The crew of the *Maggie* were expecting the steamer to go straight off from the Narrows as ships did which were going across the Atlantic. However, the *Tiber* kept close to the south side of the entrance and when outside, started to turn towards Cape Spear. It was at that point that things started getting very serious. The vessels were now getting dangerously close to each other and the people on the schooner started shouting to the steamer to keep clear. Then came a terrible crash as the *Tiber* smashed into the starboard side of the *Maggie*, cutting right through, taking the stern clean off. If the schooner had managed to get ten more feet ahead, the collision would have been avoided. The spars were taken off the schooner by the shock and she soon filled with water and sank.

When the collision occurred, panic and pandemonium ensued as 18 men and 5 women struggled for their lives in the icy, dark water among the wreckage. The horror of that scene can only be imagined as the terrified screams and pleas for help rang out over the waters of St. John's Bay. Some of the men and most of the women were in the cabin and may have been crushed to death. Those in the water clung to whatever piece of wreckage they could find; a few sank almost immediately and drowned. The first mate, Power and Moses Leithbridge grasped each other over a bundle of hay. As they struggled, the bundle rolled and Leithbridge told Power to let him go and when he did, Power was drowned. Some people were dragged under by the falling sails and spars.

The captain's wife went under the foresail and he struggled in vain to keep her up.

Two men, boarded the Tiber without getting wet and managed to get up on the leash of the foresail. Stephen Blundon caught a rope over the Tiber's side and swung out on it. Thomas Abbott had swung out on him, keeping him down by his weight. Diamond reached down, grabbed him by the collar and pulled him up to safety. But Abbott lost his hold and sank into the sea and drowned. A boat had been launched from the *Tiber* and took aboard most of those saved; a Brigus schooner saved the rest. Thirteen persons drowned in that terrible tragedy just outside the Narrows.

The survivors were brought into port and taken to the East End police station and the *Tiber's* boat returned to the steamer waiting out in the bay, which then resumed her journey. The rescued were treated very kindly and dry clothing given them. The next day an official enquiry was opened before Judge Conroy. Warrants were issued for the arrest of Captain Delisle, the mate and the lookout man of the S.S. *Tiber*, when the vessel returned from Sydney.

For the next couple of weeks, the local papers carried items relating to the *Maggie* tragedy. The death roll was also given:

Thomas Abbott, 20, married; no children
William Ash, 50, married; 9 children
Annie Blundon, 60, wife of the master and mother of a large family
George Blundon, 23, single
Joseph Diamond, 35, married; 2 children
William Diamond, 73, married; 5 children and brother of Capt. Levi Diamond
Sarah Gullage, 50, married; 3 children
Herbert Holloway, 18, single
Isabella Holloway, 20, single
Christopher Lethbridge, 24, married; 2 children
Moses Lethbridge, 33, married; 5 children
James Power, 28, married; no children
Rhoda Power 20, married; no children, wife of James Power

None of the bodies were ever recovered from the water.

SURVIVORS of the MAGGIE DISASTER - 6 NOVEMBER 1896

9 OF THE 10 SURVIVORS

*This photo was taken shortly after the **MAGGIE** disaster in the Narrows on 6 November 1896. Only 9 of the 10 survivors appear in this photo. One of the 10, Captain Blundon's 20 year old son Levi, who was very ill with tuberculosis, had been taken to the hospital shortly after being plucked from the wreckage.*

The above survivors are: Back row - l to r: Isaac or Stephen Blundon, Julius & Clara Lane, Isaac or Stephen Blundon and David Diamond; Front row - l to r: Andrew Lethbridge, Capt. William Blundon, James Lethbridge and Tom Holloway.

Photo courtesy of Fred Diamond, a son of survivor David Diamond, in top right of this photo. Fred Diamond and Fred Hancock, with the help of the late Dorothy Coultas, a grand - daughter of survivor Andrew Lethbridge, identified the above. Photographer was James Vey, St. John's.

(Photo credit Florence Cowan)

The *Tiber* was allowed to continue on its journey after the fatal accident and it nearly ran down another vessel shortly after. Captain Candow arrived in port at midnight and reported having had a narrow escape from being run down by the *Tiber* while rounding Cape Spear. Candow had all his lights up and had to light torches in order to try to attract the attention of the look-out on the steamer. Even that had no

The following poem related to the tragic ***LOSS OF THE MAGGIE*** *was taken from* ***The Treasury of Newfoundland Stories*** *published by Maple Leaf Mills Ltd. sometime in the late 1950s or early 1960s. The author's name was not included [personal copy].*

THE LOSS OF THE MAGGIE

Ye fishermen, who know so well
The dangers of the deep,
Come listen to a few sad lines,
And join with us and weep
For the loss of the schooner Maggie,
And thirteen precious lives
That left so many homes bereft
Of husbands, sons, and wives.

At ten forenoon, November five,
The Maggie sailed away
From happy homes near Brooklynn
In Bonavista Bay.
Light winds did waft her on course,
Light hearted was her crew.
When Friday evening off the narrows,
The city came in view.

Our hopes ran high, our hearts were glad,
We soon would tread the shore,

And turn to cash, the fruits of toil
Upon the Labrador.
The city lights did seem to greet,
And welcome us to town,
When Captain Blunden cried, my boys
A steamer is bearing down.

Think of a raging monster fierce,
Seeking his prey to get,
She bore right down on us, but we hoped
Her course would alter yet,
We shouted loud, in wild dismay,
"Too late", an awful crash;
Next moment o'er our shattered craft
The hungry waves did dash.

The scene that followed then; Oh God,
Tis branded on my brain.
Rather then would I wish to drown
Than witness it again.
When shriek on shriek did rend the air,
And men fought for their lives,
When brother saw a brother sink,
A husband saw his wife.

Of twenty-three that left their homes
On that bright sunny morn.
Thirteen poor souls were hushed in death
And never can return,
But the name of the steamer Tiber
Will fall in days to come
On the ears of the Brooklynn people
Like the sound of a funeral drum.

The Tiber just turned round the head
Close where the Maggie lay,
And just below the cabin doors
The schooner cut away,
The screeches of the drowning men
Were dismal for to hear
Far, far from home, and friends they loved
And orphan children dear.

The steamer's boats were quickly lowered,
And hastened to the wreck.
And some did scramble o'er her side
And landed safe on deck.
But out of three and twenty souls
Who sailed from Goose Bay shore,
Thirteen poor creatures sank that night
To see their homes no more.

(Courtesy of Florence Cowan)

effect, the steamer kept on coming towards him and he had to alter his course to avoid collision. The writer of that article and a similar one said it was a stupid blunder to allow the *Tiber* to continue on her way. She should have been detained and at least a sworn statement should have been taken from the mate.

Throngs of curious people traveled to the South Head to see the spot where the *Maggie* had gone down. There was nothing to see as the mainboom which had been sticking up above the water, disappeared below the surface on Saturday.

A fund was set up for the widows and the 24 fatherless children.

The Maggie tragedy continued in the news all the month of November because of another court case arising out of some men secreting wreckage from the vessel. Four men; Stewart Garland, Thomas Trenchard, Josiah Dawe and Robert Evan had picked up two boxes near Chain Rock and hidden them underneath Garland's stage at the Battery. Word got out and the police arrested the men under a section of the Wreck Act. Three of the men were charged with secreting a cash-box and remanded in the penitentiary for eight days while Garland was released The trial was followed in the paper until the conclusion on December 12th, which resulted in Trenchard, Dawe and Garland sentenced to 100 days imprisonment with hard labour.

The Narrows was once again crowded with schooners on November 11, 1896 when the R.M.S. *Assyrian* arrived at the Narrows at 4:50 p.m. She had to wait for an hour before she could steer a clear course in due to several schooners in the way. When she finally started to run in, she nearly cut through a schooner which wouldn't give way. The steamship had to stop and back, up almost going ashore when she got tangled up in the wreckage of the *Maggie*. Captain Hughes gave two notes of warning to mariners when he finally got in safely; first to avoid the wreckage near the South Head and second, small vessels should give way to larger ones which are far less maneuverable in the Narrows.

On November 9,1896, The *Tiber* arrived at North Sydney where Captain Delisle gave his account of the *Maggie* accident which differed from the one given by the survivors of schooner. The *Tiber*'s captain blamed the *Maggie* for the collision and gave a detailed account of that sad night. Captain Delisle was arrested en route to Montreal where his trial was held.

Mrs. Florence Cowan nee Blundon of St. John's, who has done extensive research on the accident came to the conclusion that no responsibility was ever determined. She shed a lot of light on the background of the crew. At the time of the disaster, in the community of Leithbridge where most of the drowning victims hailed from, a church was being built. After the deaths of so many members of their congregation the church was scaled down and dedicated to the memories of the victims. The 103 year old U. C. Memorial Church still stands in Leithbridge.

In February, 1897 the *Maggie* floated up, drifted off and ended up on the rocks at Black Head. The *Maggie* tragedy eventually faded and became part of the lore of seafaring tragedies.

The Usual Spring Activities

There was no major tragedy in 1897 as in 1896, but there were dozens of near misses. [see Appendix 4] In February and March, 1897, the harbour was frozen over again and boys were seen one day skating towards the *Portia* entering the Narrows. The S.S. *Mastiff* had to be butted and hauled through the ice as she tried to leave port on the second of March. Over a hundred men went before the ship and sawed out a channel for her. The sight of a ship under steam and canvas working through the ice while men shouted and pulled on the ropes, made many an old sealer sigh for the days that were gone.

On March 13, the Narrows was a beehive of activity as the *Gratia*, Captain Johns, arrived from Barbados. There were around 200 men helping to warp the 157 ton vessel in and clearing the ice. Pilot Charles Lewis almost drowned when he jumped from the vessel, *Little Mystery* and went up to his knees in the ice. He moved ahead and went up to his neck. Another Lewis tore off his coat and threw it to him and saved his life.

On June 4, 1897 the paper told about 'Romeo On a Rock;'

> "The schooner *Romeo*, Albert Hiscock, left here this morning for Trinity, taking a heavy cargo of salt and provisions. The wind being contrary she returned, and whilst beating in the Narrows she struck and hung on a rock inside

the "pancake." She was in stays, and the steam launch *Jennie Foote*, passing at the time, was run to her quarter, to turn her the better, and so the schooner was put on the rock. The *Romeo* was, however, soon afterwards towed off, and into port by the launch, and does not leak."[98]

Fishermen Stories

On July 6, 1897, three fishermen, Sidney Willar, George Morris and Peter Oliver had a close call with death. The next day they had a letter in the paper about their experience;

"......We left Big Black Head, with other boats, and when half way across our main peak block gave out and our storm-jib went to pieces. We had to bear up for Black Head Harbor; there we got a main peak block from Mr. John Shortall, and having a new jib on board we bent it and left for home. We came along so far under jib and reefed mainsail until we reached the Northern Head, intending to come in stays; and then she misstayed. We threw over the grapnel but it did not take hold, and, owing to the way the boat was, she soon smashed up. We barely had time to save our lives, on the Island rock, when she went to pieces, sprays going over us for three hours. Our cries were heard by Mr. Sheppard, of the lighthouse, and he manned a boat and came to our rescue, at 10 o'clock, and stood by us for two hours before he could get us off. We had to jump one by one, at intervals, before he could rescue us. He risked his life to save ours, as the sea was so high. He brought us to his house and gave us our supper, and we were treated with all kindness that could be done for us by Mr. Sheppard and his family. They gave us caps to put on as we saved nothing only what we had on when we jumped. She was a large fishing jack, and was fitted with all new sails and new gear. Our loss is a heavy one, which means over $60 to us, and all our support for the summer. Thanking you for publishing this letter........"[99]

On August 10, 1897 two fishermen thought they saw a sea serpent;

"While John Williams and P. Tracey were coming from the fishing ground at 7:30 last evening, their attention was attracted by a heavy splashing in the water about a gun shot away. They said they saw a monster denizen of the sea about 80 feet long and it made a great noise and after a few minutes disappeared."[100]

A sea serpent near the Narrows (Joey Power)

Dangerous Jobs

Early in 1898 there was a near fatality off the Narrows;

> "Mr. Tasker Cook nearly lost his life by drowning out in the Bay this forenoon, whilst boarding the S.S. *Parkmore*, in quest of a contract to supply her. He has to run many risks, as many or more, as reporters, and the wonder is that he has gone through unscathed so long. Mr. C. ran his boat for the ship's rope ladder, caught and held it, a difficult task with the ship steaming. He, however, started to ascend at the wrong time when the ship was on the crest of a wave. Consequently, when he was not quick enough, dallying a little to keep the boat to the ladder, for another person to catch, the ship came down with a plunge. He held his grip, and went down with her, till he was immersed to the neck in the icy waters. Launches and boats were quickly pointed for him, in case that he would have to relinquish his hold, but he held on tenaciously and was soon rescued."[101]

Sir Tasker Cook was later mayor of St. John's from 1921-1929. At the time of his ducking, he was probably trying to get the contract to supply the ship with meat as his father William had a butcher shop on Water Street. Tasker Cook took over the business and later went into municipal politics.

A similar accident befell one of the local pilots two weeks later on January 31st;

> "Mr. Lionel Lewis, pilot, nearly closed the book of his nautical life in an accidental manner yesterday afternoon. He took out the S.S. *Barcelona*, Capt. Campbell, bound for Halifax. At 4.30 p.m., when the ship was outside the Narrows, and just running out the bay, the captain said, 'The ship is safe; you may go now, pilot.' Mr. Lewis shook hands, and proceeded to leave. The pilot boat was a short distance off from the side of the steamer, and some ice between. Lewis made a leap from the ladder, to rest one foot on the ice, and then jump into the boat. At the same time the ladder gave way from him and his foot slipped. The next thing he was aware of was that he was struggling for life in the water, his back bobbing up against the bottom of the ship. This for a very short space of time, which seemed hours. Lewis felt a great fear of a chop from the propeller, which he thought was going to come to him at every stroke he gave striving to swim clear of the side of the ship. The next thing he realized was that he got his head over the surface of the water, and that a boat-hook was struck in the collar of his coat. This was done by his friends in the boat, who speedily hauled him on board. Then Lewis found out how he had escaped the propeller. The captain had been keeping an eye on him, and seeing him fall in had the engine reversed. The steamer did not bring up at once, but the whirling water from the reversed

propeller, tended to send him further forward. Lewis would not trouble the captain to board the ship again, for attendance, as he believed he would hold out good enough to reach home, even though the weather was so frosty. But when in near the Battery he was frozen stiff, and it was deemed expedient to bring him to Garland's house, near-by, where he received very careful attention and he is quite himself again to-day."[102]

Steamer-Schooner Collision

The seal fishery of 1898 was fraught with accidents and tragedy; many ships got stuck in the ice and many came home with little to show for their hard labours. On a dreary Sunday afternoon in late March the *Greenland* had slowly steamed in through a fog-shrouded Narrows with her hole full of corpses instead of seals. Nearly fifty men had perished on the ice in a blizzard when they became separated from their ship.

When the hunt was all over for that season, the *Labrador* returned with her sparse cargo of seals on May 2, 1898. A lot of people were down on the waterfront and up on Signal Hill to see the sealing vessel and to inquire how it fared at the seal fishery. As the vessel entered, a smaller craft was going out and the people watched in shock as they witnessed a collision which probably could have been easily avoided.

"While the S. S. *Labrador* was steaming into port last evening, she collided with the little schooner *Clara Bell*, Lineham, master, of St. Mary's. The *Clara Bell*, having obtained her clearance for the fishery, started for home last evening and was in the act of beating out the Narrows when the collision occurred near Chain Rock. The little schooner was on the starboard tack when the steamer struck her with full force on the starboard bow; the latter was steaming slowly, with less than half-speed. Fortunately the bow of the schooner was struck first, for had she been taken on broadside she would have gone down and probably lives would have been lost. As soon as the collision occurred two or three of the schooner's crew scrambled on the deck of the steamer; whilst the others held on to their vessel. The *Clara Bell* received considerable damage above the deck, namely: Foremast carried away, forward stanchions broken, jibboom gone and sails torn. She was not injured at all below the deck, and she is not leaking."[103]

A Young Life Lost in the Narrows

The biggest tragedy of the summer of 1898 was a sad drowning on Monday, August 22nd, right in the Narrows by Chain Rock;

> "Another terrible fatality happened last night out in the Narrows, by which young Miss May Holden, typewriter in the office of Mr. George Knowling, lost her life. She had gone out with her sister, Miss Bella Holden, and Mr. J. Robinson, her brother-in-law, also of Knowling's, to have a row on the harbor. When out near Chain Rock they saw the steam-tug *Favorite* coming with a vessel in tow. They did not have time to get out of the way of the tug, as they thought she was further distant than she really was. The look-out on board cried out to them to get out of the way, but as Miss Bella Holden had charge of the oars she became confused, and did not have time to row out of the steamer's course, which had to be altered to avoid running their boat down. The tow rope from the tug passed over the boat, and when it became taut it must have struck Miss Holden, who was sitting in the stern and knocked her overboard. The *Petunia* coming up now, to make matters worse, ran into the little boat, and destroyed, in the confusion, any chance of saving the girl's life. Cries were heard by the crew of the *Petunia*, who sang out, but received no answer. Captain Edgard, hailed to know if anyone had fallen overboard, but, receiving no reply, steamed on with his tow. The cook of the *Petunia* saw the drowning victim in the water passing by the vessel's side, and sang out to Mr. Robinson in the boat to 'Save that boy!' Seeing the white straw hat above the water, he thought it was a boy who had fallen over. No reply was given to this. Mr. Mercer, at the wheel of the *Petunia*, also saw the drowning girl floating past. When the half-dazed occupants of the boat realized the awful calamity, they were paralyzed with terror. They rowed back to land in an awful state of mind, and broke the sad news to the girl's mother, who resides on Custom House Hill. She went off in a fainting fit, and Dr.Harvey had to be called in.......The deceased was a charming and accomplished young woman, was 24 years of age, and a general favorite with all her acquaintances......"[104]

The Royal Gazette gave a similar story. However, they stated that it was the *Ingraham* which was towing in the barquentine *Petunia* and mentioned Captain Young as the captain of the tug. They said that both girls were John Robinson's sisters-in-law and that Robinson tried to remove the rope so they could get out of danger. Also, the waters were quite calm the night of the accident.

The drowning was covered in the papers for several days. Men went out searching for the body with no success. They found the woman's hat and an oar from the boat near the Southern Head. It was written that there was something very remarkable about the accident as Mr. Robinson was an extraordinary good swimmer. Perhaps the writer felt that he should have dived into the water and located her that night.

Two days after the accident a schooner was coming in the Narrows and the crew saw something floating in the middle of the Narrows. One of the crew thought at first it was a bundle of clothing and the captain thought it was a man's body. But not knowing about the drowning a couple of days previous, he too figured it must be some refuse thrown overboard by a ship and came on in without investigating. At that time, a tide was going out the Narrows at the rate of four knots per hour. The same day, diver Butler went diving around the *Petunia* seeing if he could find any trace of the missing woman; he was unsuccessful. A magisterial inquiry was held two days after the drowning.

The coverage of the Holden drowning gradually faded away. The local papers commenced reporting about other activities in and around the Narrows. [See Appendix 4]

Chain Rock Battery and the Chain Rock in the Narrows, c., 1890 (PANL)

A Barque in Danger

On November 25, 1898, *The Evening Telegram* told about a difficult time the pilots had trying to get a barque in through the Narrows;

> "The iron barque *Charlotte Young*, 302 tons, Capt. J. Ratcliffe, entered port at 2 a.m. to-day, through dense fog, without the assistance of a tug........She arrived off here on Tuesday in the midst of a dense fog, and it is a wonder how she managed to enter port. Pilot Vinnicombe boarded her at 11 o'clock last night just beyond the Narrows, and had it not been that the ship is most easily handled, and the pilots had not been there at the time, she would have collided with the Southern Head, and would have been broken to pieces by the tremendous sea. There was no wind at the time, and everything was as black as could be. It was over two hours from the time the ship entered the Narrows till she anchored opposite Baine Johnston & Co's premises on the Southside. Once in the Narrows, owing to the tide, she turned broadside, and matters began to look serious. The captain has never been here before, and he deserves great credit for bringing his ship through unscathed. Vinicombe and the other boatmen also merit great praise for their laborious efforts and good judgement."

A Storm Tossed Year

The final year covered in this book, 1899, was a storm tossed one with many lame ducks (disabled vessels) entering port. It started off early with the *Mary* on January 5th, being towed in;

> "The little schooner that was towed in yesterday afternoon with her sails blown away was the *Mary*, owned by Cashin of Cape Broyle. She was coming here with a cargo of fish when she was suddenly struck by a squall, which carried away her mainsail and damaged the other sails. There was another schooner outside the Narrows all morning with some of her sails gone. The heavy gale now raging has caused considerable damage. The *Lady Glover* was dispatched to render assistance, but up to 2 p.m. had not reached her. The three-masted schooner that was in the offing last evening has not yet arrived. She was driven away to sea and much have had a hard time last night. Little boats that are obliged to come on here at this time of the year should be provided with good gear."[105]

Three days later, two strange steamers were sighted outside, one towing another which was disabled. About 10:00 a.m., they entered the

Narrows and it was seen that the disabled ship was the S.S. *Hestia* and the S.S. *Anglian* was towing her. When the *Hestia* was nearly safe at her anchorage just inside the Narrows near Baine Johnston, her anchors dragged in the raging wind. She drifted and her stern grounded on the Southside below Baine Johnston. She damaged the S.S. *Panther* as she drifted pass and the *Anglian* nearly went ashore trying to help the *Hestia* get free. Two tugs came to her rescue and couldn't succeed in getting her off the shore that day. The *Hestia* had been three days at sea disabled before the *Anglian* answered her distress signals. The *Hestia* was very light and bringing her into St. John's was considered a triumph of seamanship. It wasn't until two days after her grounding that the tugs managed to get the *Hestia* off the Southside shore.

Lame ducks were always a source of interest for the people of St. John's and the *Bulgaria* was no exception. The S. S. *Bulgaria* was a curiosity because of her immense size, twice that of the *Anglian* which was the largest passenger ship to enter port at that time. She entered port under a misconception;

> "The S.S. *Bulgaria* entered port yesterday afternoon without a pilot. Angel's launch *Nelly*, with Dockmaster Cooksley, Messrs. J. Angel and Noseworthy, went out to meet the steamer in the Narrows. The launch, on seeing the greyhound, turned round again and steamed slowly towards the harbor, with the hope that some of its occupants might be able to board the big ship. Capt. Schmidt followed the little steamer, thinking that she was a steam pilot boat. Every turn the launch took the *Bulgaria* would take the same. Cooksley was not long before he got on deck, and as soon as he did the mate of the ship congratulated him upon bringing the vessel in so quickly and safely. The captain and officers really thought that he was a pilot, by the big French overcoat which he wore."[106]

The Bugaria was going from Hamburg to New York when she ran short of coal and that was the reason she was in St. John's. She was 11,000 tons and 500 feet long. When she was hauled into the Coastal Company wharf for coaling, hundreds of people visited her.

Triple Drowning in the Narrows

On May 1, 1899 the following tragedy occurred in the Narrows;

> "Richard Nolan, master of the schooner *Orange Bride*, Salmonier, made a deposition at the Central District Court to-day before the magistrate to the following effect: He, with his crew and four passengers, left Salmonier the 29th (Saturday). On Monday, May 1st, the skiff *Mary Francis*, of North Harbor, St. Mary's Bay, containing the three Power brothers was overtaken by the *Orange Bride* off Petty Harbor. At 3.30 on same evening they entered together, the *Orange Bride* being a little ahead. About three parts of the passage of the Narrows had been made when the crew of the *Orange Bride* missed the skiff, and on looking around carefully saw no sign of her after. There was a string of ice across the Narrows, and the *Orange Bride* got stuck in it and had to haul out to get clear, and took the weather side of the ice coming in. A heavy squall of wind struck the *Orange Bride* at this time, and the same squall striking the little skiff *Mary Jane* must have turned her over, and Capt. Nolan is very much afraid that the poor fellows met a sudden death and a watery grave in the Narrows."[107]

For a while, people held out hope that the three Power men had sought shelter in some other harbor. But hope eventually faded and they were added to the long list of those unfortunate persons who died in and around the Narrows. A fund was set up to help the family back home in North Harbour. In August, a sum of $10.00 was sent from the ladies of Tilt Cove for the Power family who lost their three sons, "last Spring by upsetting their boat near the Narrows."

The summer of 1899 saw a few upsets in the Narrows. However, there wasn't any major shipping accident. On August 9, 1899, another St. John's harbour pilot died. Samuel Ryan , aged 62 years died of paralysis. The writer noted that it was remarkable that nearly all the pilots who have died lately have died of paralytic attacks. He felt it was due to the hardship and exposure in all kinds of weather in the Narrows. Also, he stated it was time to get a steam launch for the pilot service which would be larger and offer more shelter than the current boats. It would be a "wise and humane regulation." Captain J. Callahan of the brigantine *Bella Rosa*, was chosen by the Commissioners of Pilots to replace Samuel Ryan.

On August 15th, there was another serious collision outside the Narrows;

"A serious collision between two schooners occurred last night off Small Point Bight, east of Signal Hill. A small schooner from Heart's Delight, laden with fish and manned by three men, was bound to Saint John's. When off the above-mentioned place the light of another schooner was seen apparently just under the land. To all appearances the craft was anchored and those on board the other schooner believed her to be stationary. The vessel, however, bore down upon the Heart's Delight boat and sheered along by her side, carrying away the latter's mainmast, mainsail and a lot of gear on deck and about the jibboom. The little vessel had great difficulty in reaching port. Her crew do not know the name of the craft with which they came in contact. She did not remain to see whether the crew were safe, but pursued her course without any delay. The matter will probably come under the notice of the Admiralty Court."[108]

Lost in the Narrows

As the year 1899 was winding down there were a couple of more shipping mishaps in the Narrows. The following story was told on Monday, October 23rd;

"The schr. *Phoenix*, David Hopkins, master, had a fine time along to the Narrows after leaving Old Perlican at 7 o'clock on Saturday morning last. When coming in the Narrows the rudder wheel came out of the socket, and the little twenty-five ton schooner began to drift in on the rocks between the lighthouse and Pancake Rock. The sails were lowered and both anchors dropped, but before they brought up the little vessel was pounding on the rocks. The crew, consisting of the skipper and seven men, ran and launched out the boat, and barely had time to get into her when the deck was submerged, and the seas breaking over the doomed schooner. She soon settled down in the water, and only the tops of her masts were visible. The men had no time to save anything. One man on board had $200 in cash in his chest in the cabin, but he knew it would be a risk to his life to attempt to save the money. They rowed on board the warship *Comus*, and the launch went out to the spot, but it was too late to do anything. The crew of the lost schooner walked in the cold grey of the morning to the Central Fire Station, where they were advised to go to the Seaman's Home. The vessel and cargo were uninsured, and will be a total loss to the skipper and crew, three of whom were passengers coming to buy up their winter's provisions."[109]

This last news item, taken from *The Evening Telegram* on Saturday, December 2, 1899, was titled, 'Ran On The Rocks';

"The little schooner *Maiden Bower*, of about 20 tons register, owned and commanded by Samson Rowe, of Catalina, ran on the rocks in the Narrows

A schooner stranded on Pancake Rock (Joey Power)

yesterday afternoon. She left Catalina early yesterday, and had a fine run to the Narrows, where she misstayed and ran ashore. A heavy sea was running at the time and she grounded heavily. She began to leak badly, and the crew, just after having abandoned her, found that she was driving off the shore. A tug afterwards went to the schooner's assistance, and succeeded in towing her into the harbor. The bowsprit, jibboom and part of her keel are gone, and she leaks very badly. She has on board a load of dry fish, the most of the season's catch, and it is feared that it is badly spoiled with water."

As stated at the beginning of this book, many accidents, drownings, etc., no doubt have been missed and so not included here. However, the numerous incidents (over 200) that are compiled only goes to show what a busy, dangerous and important piece of waterway the St. John's Narrows was. It is probably one of the most historic stretches of water in Canada, for certain in Newfoundland.

A picture of the Narrows taken from a postcard (CNS)

APPENDIX 1

A partial list of shipping accidents in and around the Narrows from 1813-1837

1813, May 22	*General Wellefley*, Captain Motley, struck ice while leaving harbour and sank
1813, May 22	*Hope*, Captain Banner struck South Battery and sank, crew saved
1813, December 25	*Bellona*, Captain Langlois, stranded on Prosser's Rock
1814, November 15	*Five Sisters*, Captain Smith, driven ashore at South Battery, crew escape with much difficulty
1815, May 16	brig *Vigilant*, Captain May, driven on North Head by ice and sank, no lives lost
1815, October 28	brig *Brothers*, Captain Kearney, drifted against North Head and went to pieces, no lives lost
1816, September 2	fishing boat upset in Narrows, Joseph Cooke and three men drown, two crew saved
1817, July 10	boat upset in Narrows, three men drown
1817, July 10	boat struck North Head and went to pieces, people saved
1817, August 16	schooner *Fame*, Master Johnston, upset by squall off Cuckhold's Head, crew rescued by men from South Battery
1817, August 16	boat upset off harbour and lost, all hands perished
1829, October 28	schooner *Gleaner*, master Daly, struck South Head, filled with water, later towed into harbour
1830, January 18	schooner *Providence*, Captain Murdon, struck Pancake Rock, no damage
1834, February 6	brigantine *Sophie*, cargo of oil, on fire in Narrows, one man died
1837, March 20	sealing schooner *William & Ann*, Master Knight, struck Prosser's Rock, later sunk outside Narrows, crew escaped in boats

APPENDIX 2

A partial list of shipping accidents in and around the Narrows from 1849-1870

1849, May 3	brigantine *Arabella*, Captain Price, deliberately ran ashore in Blackhead Bay after it caught fire, vessel burnt to water's edge, crew escaped
1850, September	boat belonging to Henry Pippy wrecked in Deadman's Bay, crew lost
1853, May 17	skiff upset off Blackhead, 7-9 men lost
1855, May	brigantine *Wilford Fisher*, Captain Benson, struck in Hay Cove and sunk to water level, later towed into port
1855, June 1	boat struck Cahill's Rock and sunk
1856, October 17	boat owned by Thomas Gosse struck Pancake Rock, sunk
1856, November	*Leader* struck Pancake Rock and filled
1863, March 31	western boat hit ice in Narrows and sank with all sails set, crew escaped
1863, May 9	trap-skiff, Henry Chafe owner, capsized outside entrance, pilot Vinnicombe haul men out of water
1864, June	James Neal drowned near Chain Rock when boat capsized
1866, June 5	steamer *Ashuelot* cut down brig *Selina*, Master Spracklin, off Narrows, one man Pomeroy drowned
1866, October 27	cable steamer *Hawk*, Captain Halpin, run down schooner *Norval*, Saint, Owner, in Narrows, crew saved
1869, March	*Magic*, Master Jackman, struck North Head, later towed back in
1869, July 3	Pilot James Power drowned in Narrows when hit by boom and knocked overboard from the *Marie Louise* which he was bringing in
1870, April 30	schooner *Phoca*, Master Honeywell, wrecked in Narrows, a man named Ryan was drowned
1870, November 2	HMS *Niobe* ran down schooner *Rival* from Hant's Harbour

APPENDIX 3

A partial list of shipping accidents in and around the Narrows from 1872-1887

1872, December 24	Brigus schooner *Magnolia* wrecked in Freshwater Bay, Captain W. Piercey and crew lost, one man saved
1876, October 15	brigantine *Julia*, stranded on Chain Rock and wrecked, cargo destroyed
1879, January 4	schooner *Marie*, owner David Sclater, lost in St. John's Bay, crew saved
1879, August 21	schooner *Ontario* collided with another schooner outside Narrows, both damaged and returned to port
1880, August 21	English schooner *Lilly* collided with French schooner *Provedence* while both entering Narrows
1881, May 19	steamer *Rowlands* cut down schooner off Wash Balls, tug tow schooner in
1882, January 24	schooner *Ada* hit the rocks on north side of Narrows, towed off
1883, May 12	schooner *Patriot*, Patrick Ryan (owner), wrecked inside Pancake Rock
1883, October 11	American schooner *Anniola* crashed into barquentine *Susan*, Captain Brien, in Freshwater Bay, much damage to latter vessel, crews safe
1885, August 25	banker *Aaron Perkins* aground on Cahill's Rock, floated off later
1885, November 29	schooner *Family Trial*, owner Simon Manuel, collided with a Burin craft just off Narrows, schooner damaged
1887, May 4	western boat from Renews blown over by squall of wind near Pancake Rock, men rescued off side of boat
1887, May 23	Job Brother's schooner *Delta*, William Jeans, Master, hits Southern Head, rolled off and submerged, crew escaped
1889, December 1	schooner *Hyacinth*, Josiah Manuel, owner, ashore near Chain Rock

APPENDIX 4

A partial list of accidents in and around the Narrows from 1890-1899

1890, May 17	boat laden with wood over turn in Narrows, men pulled from water
1890, October 12	man knocked overboard from Bonavista schooner, drowns in Narrows
1890, October 29	schooner *Mary*, Cashin owner, hits rocks in Hay Cove, minor damage
1890, December 3	schooner *Emmeline*, wrecked on rocks below Fort Amherst lighthouse
1891, June 16	American schooner *A. R. Crittendon*, grounded on Pancake Rock
1891, July 6	schooner *Mayor Jones*, grounded on Pancake Rock
1891, October 14	Carbonear schooner *Anna Belle*, and St. John's schooner *Messenger*, collide in Narrows
1891, November 10	Carbonear schooner *Ripple*, Captain Pike, run into by another schooner off Narrows, both return to port
1891, November 26	steamer *Portia* struck schooner *Albert*, Captain Newhook, in Narrows no damage to either vessel
1892, May 9	Keels, Bonavista schooner *Premier*, Captain Philip Fitzgerald, struck Pancake Rock, no damage
1893, September 11	banking schooner, *Grace Carter*, James Baird, owner, ran on Cahill's Rock, towed off by tug, *Favourite*
1895, October 26	schooner *Rosalind*, struck land near Hay Cove, later towed in
1896, June 10	Carbonear schooner *Emily*, Arthur Parsons, Master, grounded on Cahill's Rock, little damage
1896, June 13	*S. M. Lake*, Captain Rumsey, collided with craft, LeDrew, Master, in Narrows, latter vessel damaged
1896, August 1	schooner *Pansy*, and Heart's Content schooner *J. S. Grandy*, William Hopkins, Master, collide in Narrows, both badly damaged
1896, August 1	Lunenberg banking schooner *Malabar*, Captain William Zink, struck Pancake Rock, towed off by tug *Favourite*

1896, August 18	yacht collides with English schooner in Narrows
1896, November 10	barquentine *Nelly*, Captain R. Sheppard, and Brigus schooner *David M. Hilton*, Burke, Master, collided in Narrows, both damaged
1896, November 10	Salvage schooner *Jasper* and Pool's Island schooner *Daisy*, collide north of the Narrows, both greatly damaged
1897, April 6	boat capsize near North Head, two men, Benson and Stamp saved
1897, May 13	two St. Mary's schooners collide in Narrows in thick fog
1897, May 31	Conception Bay schooner *Swan*, John Wade, Master, collide with vessel near Chain Rock, much damage to both
1897, June 3	Pouch Cove craft, Eli Langmead, owner, collide with Trinity schooner *Lady Glover*, William Butler, Master
1897, June 16	skiff overturn in Narrows, two boys Healy and Power, rescued
1897, August 27	Quidi Vidi fishing boat upset by Chain Rock, rescued by Mr. King from Southside
1898, June 13	tug *Favourite* towing in schooners *Daisy* and *Salvationist*, rope foul in tug's propeller, one schooner collide with tug, damage to schooner
1898, November 3	two-mast schooner collide with smaller one by Southern Head, both nearly on shore, both towed in by tug *Ingraham*
1898, November 18	Lunenberg schooner *J. M. Young*, aground in Hay Cove, in heavy sea, towed in
1899, July 6	fishing boat run into by a small skiff, boat considerably damaged
1899, July 17	boat capsized by squall near Chain Rock, occupants thrown in water, one swam to shore, one rescued by fishermen

APPENDIX 5

Other events and incidents in and around the St. John's Narrows

On April 1, 1702, John Dunstan drifted out the Narrows in a small boat with no oars or sails. He was never seen again.

On April 15, 1862, the body of Andrew McGill was found in the water near Chain Rock.

On December 29, 1862, there was an explosion at the Fort Amherst batter when gun powder used to fire the fog gun, accidentally ignited.

In November, 1864, the body of a man was picked up outside the Narrows. It was believed to be a fisherman named Boul who had drowned in the Narrows the previous August.

In May, 1865, Corporal Downy was injured while blasting rock at the Fort Amherst battery. He died in July from tetanus, leaving a young family.

On September 8 & 9, 1880, the Merlin Rock was blasted by men off the *HMS Druid*, that reduced the rock to 28 feet clearance.

On August 21, 1883, men from the *HMS Canada* blasted 8 feet off the Merlin Rock so that it had 27 feet, 8 inches clearance at low tide.

On June 28, 1884, two fishermen nearly drowned when boat capsized near the Fort Amherst lighthouse. They were rescued by a tug boat.

On August 18, 1884, a violent thunder and lightning storm wreaked havoc with boats on the local fishing ground. Two men were thrown high and dry upon the beach at Blackhead.

In May, 1885, the St. John's Swimming Club had removed the bathing-house at Chain Rock, constructed a path around the cliff there to Battery Point. There the water was clearer and deeper for diving and not as rough in stormy weather as at Chain Rock. The club was looking for men to join up and help pay for a new bathing house and diving board. Up to October 3rd a dozen or so men were swimming/bathing there although the temperature of the air and water was 52^{0}.

On August 17, 1885, two fishermen found the body of Kenneth McCrithie by Chain Rock. The Cape Breton man had drowned in the harbour the night before. He left a wife and four children.

In November, 1886, 2 oxen and 5 sheep were floating on the waters outside the Narrows. The Inspector of Meats had discovered the animals perishing on board a ship in port and ordered they be taken outside the heads and thrown overboard to "put an end to their suffering." Did they shoot them first?

On August 16, 1887, large schools of herring entered the Narrows and about three barrels were caught along the Southside and at the Dock which was right up in the far end of the harbour.

On August 2, 1889, the men were out "bathing" near Chain Rock when a shark was spotted by a man who wa out rowing in a small boat. The shark came close to the side of his boat.

On May 13, 1890, an aid to help ships in distress was demonstrated in the city. R. H. Earle fired two shells as the *Volunteer* was sailing out the Narrows. The explosion was very loud and could be heard a long distance at sea. The invention was named "Earle's Distress Shell."

On May 12, 1890, a child named Rodgers fell over Signal Hill into Ross's Valley. Though he wasn't dead when picked up, little hope was given for his recovery.

On Regatta morning at 7 o'clock, July 28, 1890, the signalman on Signal Hill, Michael Cantwell, felt two shocks of an earthquake. Each shock lasted two seconds and they were twenty seconds apart.

December 3, 1890, the Battery Bathing House seen floating up harbour in storm.

On January 26, 1891, there was a serious fire at Ryan's fishing property in the Narrows. A second fire occurred there with much los of property and goods, on August 12, 1891.

On June 10, 1891, American bankers gathering ice off huge iceberg near Narrows. On June 20, the *HMS Pelican* was out firing guns at same iceberg.

The seas were heavy on October 21, 1892, striking the northern and southern heads and ascending as high as the lighthouse. The mouth of the Narrows was white with foam and the new Bathing house erected by Messrs. Lindberg Marriott & Co., at a cost of $150.00 floated out through the Narrows to sea.

The bathers were still swimming on November 8, 1892, when to their horror they discovered three dead cows in their little cove near Chain Rock. The dead cattle was thrown overboard from the cattle steamer *Ontario*.

Mr. Charles Lewis, master branch pilot of St. John's struck up a conversation with a lady passenger while piloting an Allan steamer one day. Their friendship led to an engagement and they were married on June 14, 1893, by Rev. A. C. F. Wood.

On January 23, 1894, the fog horn at Cape Spear was continuously sounding. Some of the pilots ,believing that a ship was in distress, kept a vigil in vain. The horn was blowing because James Cantwell had died and they were letting their friends in Petty Harbour know.

On May 1, 1894, the Block House up on Signal Hill burned down.

On Sunday, October 7, 1894, Mr. Thomas Sheehan of the Battery Road walked out towards Chain Rock and sat down by the little swimming cove there. Much to his horror, he discovered the body of Richard B. Peters. He ran to the nearby house of the Baker family and then reported the find to the police. It was surmised that the victim fell over the cliff.

On May 28, 1895, pilot James Furlong, 50 years old, was on duty by the pilot's quarters near the Lighthouse (Pilot's Bank), standing watch from 2-4 a.m. When he was awakened next morning, it was discovered that he was badly paralyzed. He died a week later.

On Monday, May 18, 1896, as the crew of the tug *Ingraham* were cruising outside the heads, they shot and killed a 530 pound polar bear in Freshwater Bay.

In August, 1896, Mr. Cantwell's cow fell (or jumped) over the cliff at Cape Spear and died.

On January 6, 1897, William Vinicombe died at age 82. The late master pilot had served over half a century in the pilotage service of St. John's.

On March 29, 1897, a group of boys were up on Signal Hill watching for sealing ships when one of them named Gallagher, fell into Ross's Valley. He stopped in a snowpile and was rescued and restored. A month later, a young boy named Dwyer fell 200 feet into the valley and was rescued by a man named Webber.

On April 1, 1896, two boys got trapped on a piece of ice which was going out the Narrows. They were using two brooms as oars but could not make any progress against the tide. Two men from the Southside launched a dory and rescued them a quarter of a mile outside Chain Rock.

On April 13, 1897, a man Whelan left Hoylestown to go shooting bullbirds. He walked as far as Chain Rock over the ice, shot his gun, fell on the ice and the top of his left thumb was completely blown off and his face badly injured by the gunpowder.

On June 25, 1897, the swimming season opened at Chain Rock; water temperature, 46^0 F. Up on Signal Hill the day before, the foundation stone for Cabot Tower was laid.

In December, 1897, the *S.S. Virginia* Lake arrived with 145 dogs destined for the Klondike. The schooner *Polar Bear* came in with 185 dogs. Shortly after their arrival, dogs around St. John's started disappearing.

On July 14, 1898, two men rowed in through the Narrows in an exhausted condition. They had been fishing on the Grand Banks from the *Josephine Anna* from France. They got separated in a fog and were astray for 22 days with little food or water. Marionne Lucien and Nicol Hugen were taken to the French Consul who arranged for their passage home.

On December 15, 1898, the Telephone Company connected Cape St. Francis, Cape Spear and Fort Amherst with the Central Police Station.

On July 6, 1899, J. Leamon and R. Dwyer discovered the body of Patrick Quinn out by Cuckhold's Cove. Quinn had mysteriously disappeared from his home on March 25 last.

On October 13, 1899, a horse was found dead in Ross's Valley.

On September 20, Captain Traynor in a dory named *Harold T. Bibber* left to go to Queenstown. Three years before he died he had crossed the Atlantic in a dory called *City of Bath*.

APPENDIX 6

The following article was taken from *The Evening Telegram*, June 11, 1959. It shows the competitive spirit of the early sailing captains and crews.

In the year 1896 a spirited race between Newfoundland vessels took place from St. John's to Pernambuco in Brazil. The race began Nov. 30 and featured "six smart clippers" named the *Clutha, Sunbeam, Corisande, May, Cory, Petunia*, and *Silver Sea*. Just before they sailed Captain Joyce of the *Clutha* made the remark that his vessel would get to Pernambuco at least a week ahead of the others. This remark only added spice to the race.

One of the vessels, the *Sunbeam*, had a head start. She left on the 28th, two days before the others. Four weeks went by. Then word was received in St. John's by Baine Johnston & Co. Ltd. that their vessel *Corisande*, Captain William Hughes, had reached Pernambuco. He arrived early Sunday, December 27, 1896, taking just three days under four weeks to go more than 4,000 miles. It was considered a good passage for that season of the year.

At the time the report of the *Corisande's* arrival came to St. John's no word had been heard from the *Sunbeam*, which had the head start. Captain Joyce of the *Clutha* had been left far behind in spite of his boast It was pointed out that Captain Hughes was a real "driver" of a skipper, a real record breaker. Shortly before leaving for Brazil he had sailed from Harbour Grace, to Greenock, Scotland, in ten days and returned to Harbour Grace against head winds in sixteen days. They added up to twenty-six days for the round-trip, not counting loading and unloading.

APPENDIX 7

The following was taken from the *Atlantic Guardian* for August 1952 and it tells about a curious custom called the Let-Pass around the turn of the 18th century.

The Let-Pass

The Narrows of St. John's is one of the most historic strips of water in the island of Newfoundland. In and out of it have sailed all sorts of ships, caravels, galleases, frigates, galleys, barques and brigs, men-of-war and ships of peace, merchantmen, sealers, fishing schooners. And for all we know a thousand years ago the sunlight off the Narrows may have gleamed in the shields hung along a Viking's rail.

This historic Narrows was almost always well-defended and when it was no enemy dared attack. When it was relatively unprotected, the port of St. John's was raided and captured, twice by the Dutch, half-a-dozen times by the French. On both sides of the Narrows stand the ruins or the sites of ancient forts - the Queen's Fort on Signal Hill, Fort Waldegrave and the Battery just below it; on the other side Fort Amherst and Fort Frederick and the South Fort or "The Castle."

"The Castle" contained the capstan by means of which the heavy chain that blocked the Narrows was raised or lowered as occasion required. The other end of the chain was firmly fixed to a large rock on the Signal Hill side which is still known today as Chain Rock.......

We have not mentioned Fort William which formerly stood on the site of the Newfoundland Hotel. It was the oldest fort in St. John's and one of the oldest strong points in North America dating back to very early in the 17th century. Fort William with its batteries commanded the Narrows on a direct line, and it was from its walls that the cannon of the "Let-Pass" was maintained.

The custom started back in 1776, the year of the American Revolutionary War outbreak, and it was described by antiquarians as a "queer practice." It seems that a document called the "Let-Pass" was signed by the Governor of that time, Admiral Montague, and sent to the Commanding Officer at Fort William to enable vessels to sail out of St. John's. It instructed the fort's Commander to "let the ship pass" hence the term the "Let-Pass." Such a document was apparently required in the case of each ship sailing from St. John's and certified that all Customs and Port Charges had been paid.

If the "Let-Pass" was not received by the Commanding Officer and the ship attempted to leave port, the artillery in the fort would be trained on the delinquent ship and personnel, and a warning shop fired to bring her to. In 1784 a man on the brig St. Vincent was killed in the Narrows by a shot so fired from Fort William and intended to stop a ship sailing without the Fort receiving a "Let-Pass."

Eventually this sort of thing got into the Courts as do all seemingly arbitrary practices and behaviour. The case of John F. Trimingham & Co. versus Artilleryman Johnston Gaskin brought forth from Chief Justice Forbes incidentally the composer of the "Banks of Newfoundland" the following pronouncement: "A gunner cannot justify this act of firing on a vessel by order of the governor, requiring all vessels before they proceed to sea to be provided, on pain of being fired at, and compelled to pay 6s. 8d. for shot and powder."

This "queer practice" therefore came to an end on the 9th of August, 1821, after being in existence for almost half a century.

ENDNOTES

1 Memorial University of Newfoundland, MUN, Micro Fiche 28602, Bonnycastle, Sir Richard Henry, *Newfoundland in 1842*.

2 MUN, *Sir Humphrey Gilbert in Newfoundland*, David B. Quinn, Historical Society Pamphlet Number 1983

3 *The Royal Gazette*, May 3, 1810.

4 *The Royal Gazette*, December 20, 1810.

5 *The Royal Gazette*, December 5 and 12, 1811.

6 *The Royal Gazette*, December 19, 1811.

7 *The Royal Gazette*, December 26, 1811.

8 *The Royal Gazette*, June 4, 1812.

9 *The Royal Gazette*, June 4, 1812.

10 *The Royal Gazette*, March 18, 1813.

11 *The Royal Gazette*, September 28,1815.

12 Memorial University, Centre for Newfoundland Studies, *Channel Islands and Newfoundland* by C. R. Fay.

13 *The Royal Gazette*, November 12,1812.

14 *The Royal Gazette*, November 30, 1815.

15 *The Royal Gazette*, October 15,1816.

16 *The Royal Gazette*, February 11,1817.

17 *The Royal Gazette*, February, 10, 1818.

18 *The Royal Gazette*, April 1, 1818.

19 *The Royal Gazette*, August 4, 1829.

20 *The Royal Gazette*, September 8, 1829.

21 *The Royal Gazette*, June 16, 1830.

22 *The Royal Gazette*, July 5, 1831.

23 *The Star & Newfoundland Advocate*, August 11, 1842.

24 *The Star & Newfoundland Advocate*, April 2, 1846.

25 *The Royal Gazette*, September 22, 1846.

26 *The Royal Gazette*, February 8, 1848.

27 *The Royal Gazette*, May 39, 1848.

28 *TheRoyal Gazette*, August 7, 1849.

29 Memorial University, Centre for Newfoundland Studies, *Sailing Directions for the Island of Newfoundland 1851.*

30 *The Royal Gazette*, May 9, 1854.

31 *The Royal Gazette*, August 14,1855.

32 *The Royal Gazette*, September 8, 1857.

33 *The Royal Gazette*, September, 15,1857.

34 *The Royal Gazette*, October, 13, 1857.

35 *The Evening Telegram*, April 1,1920.

36 *The Royal Gazette*, April 12,1859.

37 *The Royal Gazette*, July 31, 1860.

38 *The Royal Gazette*, August 20, 1861.

39 *The Day-Book*, March 12,1862.

40 *The Day-Book*, December 30,1862.

41 *The Public Ledger*, December 31, 1875.

42 *The Royal Gazette*, September, 19, 1876.

43 *The Royal Gazette*, September, 26, 1876.

44 *The Royal Gazette*, February 19, 1878.

45 *The Royal Gazette*, September 17, 1878.

46 *The Royal Gazette*, January 7, 1879.

47 *The Evening Telegram*, July 9, 1879.

48 *The Evening Telegram*, August 6, 1879.

49 *The Evening Telegram*, August 12, 1879.

50 *The Royal Gazette*, November 11, 1879.

51 *The Evening Telegram*, February 20, 1880.

52 *The Evening Telegram*, March 30, 1880.

53 *The Evening Telegram*, April 3, 1880.

54 *The Royal Gazette*, April 6, 1880.

55 *The Royal Gazette*, April 27, 1880.

56 *The Evening Telegram*, May 18, 1880.

57 *The Evening Telegram*, June 16, 1881.

58 *The Evening Telegram*, February 7, 1882.

59 *The Evening Telegram*, April 4, 1882.

60 *The Royal Gazette*, August 22, 1882.

61 *The Evening Telegram*, May 31, 1883.

62 *The Evening Telegram*, August 31, 1883.

63 *The Evening Telegram*, June 7, 1884.

64 *The Royal Gazette*, July 29, 1884.

65 *The Evening Telegram*, August 26, 1884.

66 *The Evening Telegram*, July 30, 1885.

67 *The Evening Telegram*, October 25, 1886.

68 *The Evening Telegram*, October, 27, 1886.

69 *The Evening Telegram*, March 10, 1887.

70 *The Evening Telegram*, April 11, 1887.

71 *The Evening Telegram*, March 14, 1887.

72 *The Royal Gazette*, November 29, 2887.

73 *The Evening Telegram*, May 9, 1888.

74 *The Evening Telegram*, June 2, 1888.

75 *The Evening Telegram*, September 10, 1888.

76 *The Evening Telegram*, September 5, 1889.

77 *The Evening Telegram*, October 2, 1889.

78 *The Evening Telegram*, December 6, 1890.

79 *The Evening Telegram*, March 10, 1891.

80 *The Daily Colonist*, July 9, 1891.

81 *The Evening Telegram*, August 10, 1891.

82 *The Daily Colonist*, September 17, 1891.

83 *The Evening Telegram*, September 24, 1891.

84 *The Daily Colonist*, October 15, 1891.

85 *The Daily Colonist*, June 1, 1982.

86 *The Evening Telegram*, June 4, 1892.

87 *The Royal Gazette*, July 25, 1892.

88 *The Evening Telegram*, September 1, 1893.

89 *The Evening Telegram*, October 16, 1893.

90 *The Evening Telegram*, November 17, 1893.

91 *The Evening Telegram*, March 27, 1894.

92 *The Evening Telegram*, October 7, 1895.

93 *The Evening Telegram*, April 11, 1896.

94 *The Evening Telegram*, June 5, 1896.

95 *The Evening Telegram*, August 6, 1896.

96 *The Evening Telegram*, October 15, 1896.

97 *The Evening Telegram*, November 2, 1896.

98 *The Evening Telegram*, June 4, 1897.

99 *The Evening Telegram*, July 7, 1897.

100 *The Evening Telegram*, July 17, 1897.

101 *The Evening Telegram*, January 17, 1898.

102 *The Evening Telegram*, February, 1, 1898.

103 *The Evening Telegram*, May 3, 1898.

104 *The Evening Telegram*, August 23, 1898.

105 *The Evening Telegram*, January 6, 1899.

106 *The Evening Telegram*, January 14, 1899.

107 *The Evening Telegram*, May 9,1899.

108 *The Evening Telegram*, August 16, 1899.

109 *The Evening Telegram*, October 23, 1899.